# Causes of Cancer

# Causes of
# Cancer

**Donna M. Bozzone, Ph.D.**

Consulting Editor:
Donna M. Bozzone, Ph.D.
Professor of Biology
Saint Michael's College

CHELSEA HOUSE
PUBLISHERS
An imprint of Infobase Publishing

**THE BIOLOGY OF CANCER: CAUSES OF CANCER**

Chelsea House
An imprint of Infobase Publishing
132 West 31st Street
New York NY 10001

**Library of Congress Cataloging-in-Publication Data**
Bozzone, Donna M.
  Causes of cancer / Donna M. Bozzone.
    p.; cm. – (Biology of cancer)
  Includes bibliographical references and index.
  ISBN-13: 978-0-7910-8819-7 (alk. paper)
  ISBN-10: 0-7910-8819-7 (alk. paper)
  1. Cancer—Etiology—Popular works. I. Title. II. Series.
  [DNLM: 1. Neoplasms–etiology. QZ 202 B793c 2007]

  RC268.48.B69 2007
  616.99'4071–dc22                                    2007009174

Chelsea House books are available at special discounts when purchased in bulk quantities for businesses, associations, institutions, or sales promotions. Please call our Special Sales Department in New York at (212) 967-8800 or (800) 322-8755.

You can find Chelsea House on the World Wide Web at http://www.chelseahouse.com

Text design by James Scotto-Lavino
Cover design by Ben Peterson
Illustrations by Chris and Elisa Scherer

Printed in the United States of America

Bang EJB 10 9 8 7 6 5 4 3 2 1

This book is printed on acid-free paper.

All links and Web addresses were checked and verified to be correct at the time of publication. Because of the dynamic nature of the Web, some addresses and links may have changed since publication and may no longer be valid.

Gleevec® is a registered trademark of Novartis Pharmaceuticals Corporation; Gardasil® is a registered trademark of Merck & Co.; Herceptin® is a registered trademark of Genentech, Inc.

# CONTENTS

♦

# FOREWORD

♦

Approximately 1,500 people die each day of cancer in the United States. Worldwide, more than 8 million new cases are diagnosed each year. In affluent, developed nations such as the United States, around 1 out of 3 people will develop cancer in his or her lifetime. As deaths from infection and malnutrition become less prevalent in developing areas of the world, people live longer and cancer incidence increases to become a leading cause of mortality. Clearly, few people are left untouched by this disease due either to their own illness or that of loved ones. This situation leaves us with many questions: What causes cancer? Can we prevent it? Is there a cure?

Cancer did not originate in the modern world. Evidence of humans afflicted with cancer dates from ancient times. Examinations of bones from skeletons that are more than 3,000 years old reveal structures that appear to be tumors. Records from ancient Egypt, written more than 4,000 years ago, describe breast cancers. Possible cases of bone tumors have been observed in Egyptian mummies that are more than 5,000 years old. It is even possible that our species' ancestors developed cancer. In 1932, Louis Leakey discovered a jawbone, from either *Australopithecus* or *Homo erectus*, that possessed what appeared to be a tumor. Cancer specialists examined the jawbone and suggested that the tumor was due to Burkitt's lymphoma, a type of cancer that affects the immune system.

er has been a concern for the human lineage for at

.

have been searching for ways to treat and cure cancer

s, but cancer is becoming an even greater problem

expectancy increased dramatically in the twentieth

lic health successes such as improvements in our abil-

fight infectious disease, more people live long enough

r. Children and young adults can develop cancer, but

the chance of developing the disease increases as a person ages. Now that so many people live longer, cancer incidence has increased dramatically in the population. As a consequence, the prevalence of cancer came to the forefront as a public health concern by the middle of the twentieth century. In 1971 President Richard Nixon signed the National Cancer Act and thus declared "war" on cancer. The National Cancer Act brought cancer research to the forefront and provided funding and a mandate to spur research to the National Cancer Institute. During the years since that action, research laboratories have made significant progress toward understanding cancer. Surprisingly, the most dramatic insights came from learning how normal cells function, and by comparing that to what goes wrong in cancer cells.

Many people think of cancer as a single disease, but it actually comprises more than 1,000 different disorders in normal cell and tissue function. Nevertheless, all cancers have one feature in common: All are diseases of uncontrolled cell division. Under normal circumstances, the body regulates the production of new cells very precisely. In cancer cells, particular defects in deoxyribonucleic acid, or DNA, lead to breakdowns in the cell communication and growth control normal in healthy cells. Having escaped these controls, cancer cells can become invasive and spread to other parts of the body. As a consequence, normal tissue and organ functions may be seriously disrupted. Ultimately, cancer can be fatal.

Even though cancer is a serious disease, modern research has provided many reasons to feel hopeful about the future of cancer treatment and prevention. First, scientists have learned a great deal about the specific genes involved in cancer. This information paves the way for improved early detection, such as identifying individuals with a genetic predisposition to cancer and monitoring their health to ensure the earliest possible detection. Second, knowledge of both the specific genes involved in cancer and the proteins made by cancer cells has made it possible to develop very specific and effective treatments for certain cancers. For example, childhood leukemia, once almost certainly fatal, now can be treated successfully in the great majority of cases. Similarly, improved understanding of cancer cell proteins led to the development of new anticancer drugs such as Herceptin, which is used to treat certain types of breast tumors. Third, many cancers are preventable. In fact, it is likely that more than 50 percent of cancers would never occur if people avoided smoking, overexposure to sun, a high-fat diet, and a sedentary lifestyle. People have tremendous power to reduce their chances of developing cancer by making good health and lifestyle decisions. Even if treatments become perfect, prevention is still preferable to avoid the anxiety of a diagnosis and the potential pain of treatment.

The books in *The Biology of Cancer* series reveal information about the causes of the disease; the DNA changes that result in tumor formation; ways to prevent, detect, and treat cancer; and detailed accounts of specific types of cancers that occur in particular tissues or organs. Books in this series describe what happens to cells as they lose growth control and how specific cancers affect the body. *The Biology of Cancer* also provides insights into the studies undertaken, the research experiments done, and the scientists involved in the development of the present state of knowledge of this disease. In this way, readers get to see beyond "the facts" and understand more about the process of biomedical research. Finally, the books in *The Biology of Cancer* series provide information to help readers make healthy choices that can reduce the risk of cancer.

Cancer research is at a very exciting crossroads, affording scientists the challenge of scientific problem solving as well as the opportunity to engage in work that is likely to directly benefit people's health and well-being. I hope that the books in this series will help readers learn about cancer. Even more, I hope that these books will capture your interest and awaken your curiosity about cancer so that you ask questions for which scientists presently have no answers. Perhaps some of your questions will inspire you to follow your own path of discovery. If so, I look forward to your joining the community of scientists; after all, there is still a lot of work to be done.

**Donna M. Bozzone, Ph.D.**
Professor of Biology
Saint Michael's College
Colchester, Vermont

# 1

## An Unexpected Clue

**KEY POINTS**

◆ Cancer is a disease of uncontrolled cell division.

◆ Cancer is a major cause of death in the United States and worldwide.

◆ Cancer cells do not follow the normal rules of cell behavior.

◆ Cancer can be caused by a variety of external and internal factors.

During the course of your lifetime, the cells of your body will divide to make new cells 10,000 trillion times. In most cases, these new cells work well with other cells. All cell types—skin or blood cells, for example—have their own specific jobs. This allows the whole body, made up of tissues, organs, and organ systems, to function smoothly. Sometimes, however, a cell divides in an uncontrolled manner, producing **cancer**.

According to current estimates, approximately 40 percent of all Americans will contract cancer and half of these people will die from the disease. Even if you are fortunate and do not develop cancer yourself, it is fairly likely that someone you know will. Understanding cancer's causes can help us better prevent, diagnose, and treat this disease, which is a critical biomedical goal. Perhaps the first question to consider is whether cancer is caused by factors **intrinsic** to the cells—meaning that something goes wrong inside the cells, such as a **mutation** or error in the DNA—or **extrinsic** to the cell, meaning that the problem is caused by outside events, such as exposure to chemicals. Perhaps cancer is caused by both intrinsic and extrinsic factors.

## CHIMNEY SWEEPS PROVIDED AN EARLY CLUE

Although it has never been easy to be poor, children growing up in England in the eighteenth and nineteenth centuries had especially difficult lives. There were no child labor laws like the ones we have today, and some children—even those as young as six years old—worked 10 to 12 hours a day, often under appalling conditions as laborers in factories, coal mines, or farms. One of the worst jobs for a child was to work as a chimney sweep. Sold to a master chimney sweeper by the age of six or seven, the boys squeezed into narrow chimneys that might be only nine inches (23 cm)—or even fewer—in diameter. To make it easier for them to slide through the chimneys, the boys worked naked. Chimney sweeping was a dangerous occupation; some boys died on the job. Those who survived suffered many physical problems, including skeletal deformities, eye irritations and infections, respiratory illnesses, and eventually "soot warts," or the "chimney sweeps' cancer." This is a cancer that appears on the skin of the **scrotum**. If left untreated, it is fatal.

The high incidence of cancer of the scrotum among chimney sweeps was first reported by London surgeon Percival Pott in 1775. Pott not only described the increased frequency of this disease in chimney sweeps compared to the general population, he also detailed the progression of the cancer, and, most important, described that the skin irritated by soot as the cancer's cause. Because the young chimney sweeps worked naked and bathing was rare, the soot collected on the delicate folds of the scrotal skin and irritated it. Pott noticed that there was often a lag, or interval of time, between the exposure to soot and the eventual onset of the cancer. Based on his studies Pott made some suggestions to help prevent chimney sweeps' cancer. One recommendation was quite straightforward: bathe regularly.

The chimney sweep guild of Denmark paid attention to Pott's report and urged its members to bathe daily. French chimney sweeps also bathed more frequently than their English counterparts. The result of all of this bathing was a dramatic reduction in the incidence of chimney sweep cancer in countries other than England, which led the *British Medical Journal* to publish an article in 1892 entitled "Why Foreign Sweeps Do Not Suffer from Scrotal Cancer."

Pott's finding of an outside, or extrinsic, cause for cancer has been verified and expanded upon in the two centuries since his report appeared. Evidently things can be done *to* cells to make them become cancerous. Now it is important to consider what happens *inside* a cell that leads to uncontrolled growth and the production of a **tumor**, or abnormal mass of cells.

## HOW DO CANCER CELLS MISBEHAVE?

Even conservative estimates claim that there are probably more than 100 different types of cancer. At first glance this large number of varieties might suggest that trying to understand the cause, prevention,

## SPOTLIGHT ON CANCER SCIENTISTS
### PERCIVAL POTT (1714–1788)

Born in London, England, in 1714, Percival Pott was one of the preeminent surgeons of his day. He was the first person to demonstrate a clear relationship between the development of cancer and exposure to an occupational **carcinogen**.

Even though his father died when Pott was only three years old, Percival was raised in fairly comfortable circumstances. Thanks to his mother's relative the Bishop of Rochester, Pott was able to go to a good school. Drawn to the study of medicine, Pott was apprenticed at the age of 16 to a surgeon named Edward Nourse at St. Bartholomew's Hospital in London. Pott studied anatomy, surgery, and medical science. At the age of 23, he received a diploma for the practice of surgery, a very significant accomplishment. After completing an internship at St. Bartholomew's, Pott was appointed assistant surgeon in 1744, and became a full surgeon in 1749. A small, well-dressed (he always wore a wig), sociable man, Pott was an impressive teacher and surgeon.

and treatment of cancer is hopeless. This is not the case. Researchers have shown that, for all its variety, cancer appears to occur because of a disruption or malfunction of a small number of critical regulatory circuits that govern normal cell behavior. Cancer is a result of the improper functioning of the genetic and biochemical behaviors that cells normally exhibit.

After a fall from a horse in 1756, Pott discovered that he had another talent, writing. While recovering from a compound fracture of the tibia (shin bone), he began to write medical articles. Even after his leg healed, Pott continued to publish works based on his medical practice and surgery. Today Pott is well remembered for the account he published in 1775 called *A Short Treatise of the Chimney Sweeper's Cancer.*

**Figure 1.1** Percival Pott. (*National Institutes of Health/U.S. National Library of Medicine*)

Pott retired from St. Bartholomew's in 1788 after more than 40 years as a surgeon. He contracted pneumonia three months later and died on December 22, 1788. On the day before he died, Pott said, "My lamp is almost extinguished. I hope it has burned for the benefit of others."

For a cell to **transform** from its normal, healthy state to a **malignant**, **invasive** state involves the development of a relatively small number of abnormal cell behaviors. The process of reaching a fully malignant state is gradual and arduous. Most of the time, the body's own defenses will prevent cancer from forming, but sometimes cells can evade these internal protections.

So what are abnormal behaviors for cells? Cells become resistant to the normal cues that regulate cell division in the multistep transformation from normal to invasive and cancerous. For some types of cells, such as those producing blood or skin, frequent cell division is normal. However, cells on the way to becoming cancerous may even produce their own chemical signals to trigger cell division. Moreover these cells ignore the self-destruct orders that are generally delivered to abnormal cells. Ordinarily, cell populations have a limited lifespan. They will divide a certain number of times and then they die. Cancer cells, on the other hand, are **immortalized**, meaning that there is no limit to the number of times the cells can divide. This immortalization is quite remarkable: Cells that were isolated in the 1950s from a **cervical** cancer continue to survive today in **tissue culture**. The immortalized cells continue to live and divide, producing a population of abnormal cells.

Once a population of cancer cells in the body reaches a millimeter or so in diameter, it needs a blood supply so that it can get nutrients and oxygen and thus keep growing. If the cell transformation is far enough advanced, the developing tumor will send out chemical signals called **angiogenic factors** to attract capillaries, or very fine blood vessels. These capillaries allow the tumor to attach to the circulatory system. Once it is supplied with oxygen and nutrients, the tumor can continue to grow.

Finally some cancer cells detach themselves from the tumor and enter the bloodstream. This invasive behavior is called **metastasis**. When it occurs, new or secondary tumors can form at sites in the body that are distant from the site of the original tumor.

It is likely that billions of cells take the first step toward becoming cancerous. Fortunately other steps are also required for a full-blown malignancy to develop. Our immune systems provide significant

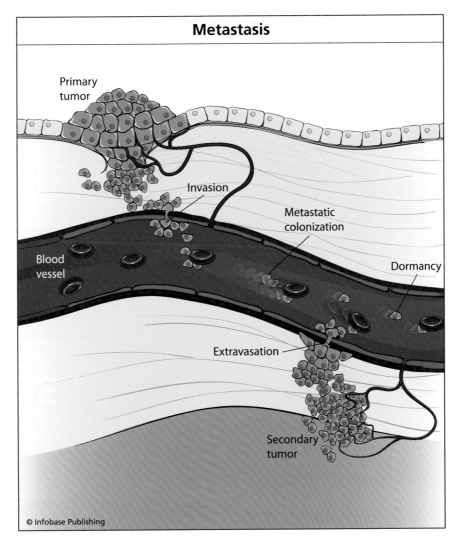

**Figure 1.2** The steps in the process of metastasis.

defenses against such developments. Consequently cancers are usually prevented or delayed. In fact we can see evidence of the behavioral "mistakes" that are committed by cells in the development of **benign** tumors that pose no danger, such as warts, or in growths that show

## SPOTLIGHT ON CANCER SCIENTISTS
### JUDAH FOLKMAN (1933– )

Judah Folkman was born in Cleveland, Ohio, in 1933. He originally thought he would become a rabbi like his father, but after visiting the hospital at the age of seven, Folkman decided he wanted to become a physician. He was drawn to a career in medicine because he wanted to devote his life to the service of others. After completing college, Folkman went to Harvard Medical School. While he was a medical student, he worked with a research team that developed the first implantable pacemaker used to control heart function.

After finishing medical school, Folkman continued his training to become a surgeon. During a two-year tour of duty in the U.S. Navy (1960–1962), he made a discovery at a government lab in Bethesda, Maryland. Folkman was studying tumor growth outside of the body in isolated organs. He noticed that tumors on the cultured organs grew to a very small size and then stopped growing—always at the same size. This was very different from what happens in the body. From this observation, Folkman realized that something was stopping the tumors in culture from growing. Folkman found that tumors can grow only to a certain size—no bigger than the head of a pin—unless they are connected to blood vessels.

**Figure 1.3** Judah Folkman. (*Steve Gilbert/Studioflex*)

He hypothesized that tumors produced chemical signals—angiogenesis (also angiogenic) factors—which cause blood vessels to grow toward them. Once connected to the circulatory system the tumor, now supplied with oxygen and nutrients, could continue to grow. Folkman reasoned that if this blood vessel growth could be prevented or reversed, then tumors would not be able to grow. Since this theory was first proposed, many angiogenesis factors have been found. Even more exciting, many angiogenesis inhibitors have also been identified. Thanks to the research of Judah Folkman and his colleagues, we may soon have a new treatment for cancer in addition to surgery, chemotherapy, and radiation therapy.

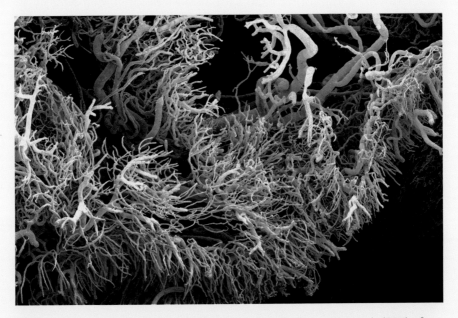

**Figure 1.4** Tumor blood vessels. Colored scanning electron micrograph (SEM) of a resin cast of blood vessels from an intestinal tumor. This branching network of vessels surrounded the tumor, supplying it with blood. Tumors are the uncontrolled growth of a tissue, and they trigger a growth of new blood vessels to supply the blood for such growth. (*CLOUDS HILL IMAGING, LTD / Photo Researchers, Inc.*)

some but not all of the changes associated with cancer formation, such as intestinal **polyps**.

## SUMMARY

It is clear from the observations of Pott and many others over the last two centuries that there are external causes of cancer. Cells are assaulted by various chemical, physical, and biological factors that can lead to cancer development. An understanding of the ways that cancer cell behaviors differ from those of normal cells leads to the conclusion that there are also internal cellular changes that result in cancer. Evidently both extrinsic and intrinsic factors are important for carcinogenesis. In fact the external triggers appear to operate by influencing the internal functioning of the cell, typically by altering its **DNA** and its genetic instructions. In the chapters that follow, we will take a close look at how to determine whether a substance or event is carcinogenic, what is known about the specific external causes of cancer, and what can be done to prevent cancer.

# 2

# HOW DO WE DETERMINE
# THE CAUSES OF CANCER?

**KEY POINTS**

- The causes of cancer are determined by using both the tools of epidemiology and experimentation.

- Epidemiology is the study of when and where diseases occur in a population.

- Epidemiology has provided information about cancer causes and strategies for prevention.

- Experimentation is important for determining the cellular mechanisms that are responsible for cancer.

- We can take action to reduce our personal cancer risk.

Shortly after her doctors told Lorraine Pace of West Islip, Long Island, that she had breast cancer, she learned that she was the 20th person in her neighborhood to be diagnosed with the disease. Was this cluster of breast cancer cases the result of some external cause, such as exposure to a carcinogenic chemical? Were all of these breast cancers the same type, triggered by a specific event, or were they caused by independent, unrelated occurrences? What caused breast cancer to develop in these 20 women?

Scientists take two general approaches to determine what causes cancer. One approach is to look at people who have been exposed to particular chemicals, microorganisms, or radiation, and see whether they develop cancer. This strategy uses the tools of **epidemiology**, the study of when and where disease occurs in a population. Another way to find out what causes cancer is to do experiments that explore the mechanisms that are responsible for turning normal cells into cancerous ones. In order to gain a full understanding of the causes of cancer for the purposes of prevention and treatment, both epidemiology and experimentation are essential.

## EPIDEMIOLOGY

As discussed in Chapter 1, English physician Percival Pott published one of the earliest accounts linking exposure to a specific carcinogenic material—soot—to the development of a specific cancer—scrotal—in a particular population—chimney sweeps. Pott was not alone in making these types of connections. In 1761, London physician John Hill proposed that inhaling "snuff" (tobacco) caused nasal cancer, and in 1795, the German physician Samuel T. von Soemmering reported that pipe smokers suffered from lip cancer more commonly than people who did not smoke pipes. It is ironic that, thanks to the Industrial Revolution of the nineteenth century, unintended experiments were done on populations of workers who were exposed to brand-new chemicals and manufacturing by-products. Some of these workers developed cancers that had been rare before the expansion of industry. In the 1930s the German physician Wilhelm C. Hueper was hired by the chemical industry giant DuPont to study whether there was a relationship between exposure to aromatic amines—chemicals produced in the company's factories—and the development of bladder cancer in workers. Hueper's studies revealed that there was indeed such a relationship. In response DuPont fired him. In all of these cases, establishing the possible links between carcinogens and the development of cancers in people was done by analyzing disease patterns in populations of exposed individuals and comparing the **incidence** of the same diseases in populations of unexposed individuals.

Epidemiology is an information science; it focuses on what is happening in populations of people rather than considering only the situation of any specific individual. Epidemiology is a very important weapon in the prevention of disease and for limiting its spread once disease is present. In the case of cancer, epidemiologists have been very successful in identifying cancer risks and causes, helping to decrease the incidence of cancer even in cases where the precise details of the cause are not clear. For example epidemiology provided evidence that smoking does indeed cause cancer.

Epidemiologists try to identify all the important factors involved in a disease, such as age, gender, socioeconomic status, occupation, personal habits, and the presence of other diseases. They collect data from censuses, statistics on births and deaths, and disease reports from sources such as the Centers for Disease Control and Prevention's

## SPOTLIGHT ON CANCER SCIENTISTS
### WILHELM C. HUEPER (1894–1979)

Born in Germany, Wilhelm C. Hueper earned his medical degree in 1920. He came to the United States shortly thereafter and worked as a pathologist in cancer research laboratories. In 1934 Hueper sent a letter to the head of the DuPont chemical company, warning him that DuPont's dye workers were being exposed to bladder carcinogens and were likely to develop bladder cancer as a result. Hueper based his theory on many reports of bladder cancer among European dye workers between 1895 and 1913. In 1921 the International Labor Office (ILO) also issued a report detailing the association between bladder cancer and working on the manufacture of dyes. DuPont hired Hueper to join its Haskell Laboratory of Industrial Toxicology.

Hueper focused his attention on trying to identify the carcinogenic chemicals in the dye works. In 1937 he induced bladder cancer in dogs by

*Morbidity and Mortality Weekly Report.* They also consult hospital records and conduct surveys. Using sophisticated statistical analysis, epidemiologists try to identify factors that play a role in the development of cancer. Since it is unethical to perform experiments on groups of people to determine causes of cancer, epidemiology provides a way to take a look back at what people have already been exposed to and then see whether cancers form. From these types of studies we have learned that the causes of cancer are quite complex and appear to be sensitive to a person's environment and cultural practices. For

exposing them to beta-naphthylamine, one of the dye components. This cancer was the same type of malignancy suffered by workers who were exposed to the same chemical. Hueper had established an animal model that would be appropriate for studying a specific human cancer. Such a model was a critical tool for studying bladder cancer to figure out how to prevent and control the disease. Hueper was the first person to combine both approaches to the study of the causes of cancer—to observe the response of a human population to a carcinogen *and* to study the effect of a carcinogen in controlled laboratory studies.

Unfortunately DuPont was not happy with Hueper's research and findings; the company fired him in 1937 and did not allow him to publish the results of the experiments he had done at DuPont. Fortunately Hueper got another job as a pathologist and continued his lifelong research on chemical carcinogens. In fact his research formed the scientific basis for the 1958 Delaney Amendment, a law that banned carcinogens from food.

example Table 2.1 on page 26 shows the incidence of five different types of cancer in Japanese people, people of Japanese origin who moved to Hawaii, and people living in Hawaii who are not of Japanese descent. The incidence of these five cancers appears to depend more on where an individual is living rather than ethnicity. For example cancer of the colon is less prevalent in Japan than it is in either of the study populations living in Hawaii. This type of information encourages scientists to examine differences and similarities in lifestyles and diet in order to identify which factor or factors are responsible for the increase in colon cancer. This same approach can be used to consider any type of cancer. The strength and benefit of epidemiology is that it allows people to identify risks so that they can prevent certain cancers by altering their behaviors. When possible, prevention is much better than trying to treat the disease, both from the perspective of human suffering and economic cost.

| TABLE 2.1   JAPAN TO HAWAII | | | |
|---|---|---|---|
| CANCER (SEX) | JAPAN | HAWAII JAPANESE | HAWAII CAUCASIAN |
| Colon (M) | 78 | 371 | 368 |
| Prostate (M) | 14 | 154 | 343 |
| Breast (F) | 335 | 1221 | 1869 |
| Stomach (M) | 1331 | 397 | 217 |
| Cervix (F) | 329 | 149 | 243 |

Source: Doll, R. and R. Peto. *The Causes of Cancer.* Oxford: Oxford University Press, 1981.

## EXPERIMENTATION

Although many cancers can be prevented or delayed, it is inevitable that some will still occur. In order to enhance our ability to prevent and treat cancer effectively, it is important to understand what happens to cells, tissues, and organs when cancer develops. In this way we can learn about the specific mechanisms that are part of cancer formation and find ways to circumvent these mechanisms to stop the uncontrolled proliferation of cells. The most powerful approach for solving these types of problems is experimentation.

The first recorded effort to deliberately induce cancer in a test animal was done by the French scientist Jean Clunet, who in 1908 showed that exposure to **X rays** caused skin cancer in rats. The way that X rays could cause cancer was made clearer by studies done in 1928 by the German-born American scientist Hermann Joseph Muller. Using the fruit fly as his study organism, Muller showed that X rays damaged DNA. As we will see in Chapter 5, some types of DNA damage can lead to cancer.

In addition to studying carcinogens such as X rays, scientists explored the chemical causes of cancer. Scientists rubbed chemicals on the skin of test animals to see if tumors could be induced. The first efforts were uniformly unsuccessful. However, in 1915, the Japanese scientists Katsusaburo Yamagiwa and Koichi Ichikawa reported the results of a careful study in which they applied coal tar to the skin of rabbit ears every two to three days for 275 days. To their surprise Yamagiwa and Ichikawa succeeded in inducing skin cancer by means of a chemical carcinogen. To commemorate the occasion and express his joy for his success, Yamagiwa composed a poem that read: "Cancer was produced! Proudly I walk a few steps."[1] In 1930, the specific carcinogenic chemical in the coal tar was identified: dibenzanthracene. This work revealed that a specific chemical could make cells become cancerous and also provided the first tools for inducing cancer formation in a controlled study. Research to identify specific chemical carcinogens continues today, although much of the screening of substances is done

## SPOTLIGHT ON CANCER SCIENTISTS
### KATSUSABURO YAMAGIWA (1863–1930)

Born in Ueda, Japan, in 1863 to parents of high social standing, Katsusaburo Yamagiwa attended his local school, exhibiting academic talent that might have gone undeveloped if he had not been adopted by a Tokyo physician who saw great promise in him. Yamagiwa was educated at Tokyo Imperial University, earning his medical degree in 1888. He specialized in pathology and rose through the ranks at Tokyo Imperial University. As an associate professor of pathology, he was sent to Germany to advance his learning. Yamagiwa worked for two years with the eminent German scientist Rudolf Virchow. Upon returning to Tokyo in 1894, Yamagiwa continued his research in cancer and other problems in pathology. He was promoted to professor of pathology and head of the department in 1895, continuing in this position until his retirement in 1923.

using tissue culture and microbiological methods rather than using live animals.

In addition to experiments that revealed the existence of both physical and chemical carcinogens, other research showed that **chromosome** defects play a part in many cancers, and that some cancers are caused by viruses. Experimentation into the causes and mechanisms of cancer development has enhanced our understanding of what happens to cells when they become cancerous. In all cases some aspect of DNA structure and function is altered in cancerous cells. Like epidemiological studies,

In the nineteenth and early twentieth centuries, when Yamagiwa was doing his work, there was a lot of speculation regarding the mechanism for carcinogenesis. Three ideas predominated: 1) Rudolf Virchow's irritation theory, which said that cancer results from the continual irritation and **inflammation** of cells and tissues; 2) Cohnheim-Ribbert's cellular hypothesis[1], which said that tumors result from "leftover" embryonic cells that do not respond to normal growth controls and keep dividing thus producing tumors, and 3) the parasite hypothesis, which proposed that malignancies are the results of specific infections or infestations. When Yamagiwa and Ichikawa successfully produced malignancies on rabbit ear skin, they provided the first evidence to support the irritation theory and, more important, ushered in a new era in cancer research. Through their careful and painstaking experiments, Yamagiwa and Ichikawa also established methods whereby other researchers could reliably produce cancer in the laboratory and study the disease in well-controlled experiments.

experimentation is an ongoing effort aimed at understanding and preventing cancer, as well as treating it.

## THE MEANING OF RISK

It is challenging to consider the vast amount of available evidence regarding cancer and to evaluate one's own personal risk for developing the disease. This is a potentially confusing task because risks are reported for populations of people rather than individuals. A lot of numbers are also reported in different ways, making the effort even more difficult. For example the risk of developing lung cancer for a regular smoker is approximately 10 to 15 percent. This means that 85 to 90 percent of smokers will *not* get lung cancer (although many will suffer from other smoking-related illnesses). For those who do not smoke, the lifetime chance of having lung cancer is less than 1 percent. In fact smoking increases the relative risk of lung cancer 10 to 40 times that of a nonsmoker. And smoking can be the cause of 87 to 90 percent of all lung cancers. What can be concluded from of all these figures? It is important to realize that epidemiologists can predict the relative risk of a particular behavior, such as smoking, based on the percentages. Your own individual outcome will either be zero percent—meaning you do not get cancer, or 100 percent—meaning you do. So out of 100 people who smoke, on average, 10 to 15 will develop lung cancer. But which ones? This is hard to predict because cancer development is influenced by many factors over the long period of time during which a transformed cell develops into an invasive tumor. Nevertheless it makes sense to look at the odds and to adjust behaviors, so that you are part of the population from which only one person out of 100 develops lung cancer (nonsmokers), rather than the population from which 10 to 15 out of 100 will do so (smokers).

Just as it can be difficult to interpret the full meaning of epidemiological evidence, it is also challenging to know how to view evidence that is gathered through experimentation. It may seem illogical or unethical to do studies aimed at determining whether a substance is carcinogenic in which experimental organisms—mice or rats, for example—are exposed to quantities far greater than anything a human might ordinarily encounter. One of the main reasons that some experiments are done this way is to establish a biologically plausible mechanism for cancer causation. Even in cases where there is firm epidemiological evidence for a particular cause of cancer, it is essential to demonstrate through experiments *how* the carcinogen actually produces cancerous cells and tumors.

Ultimately people can determine their relative chances of developing particular cancers and also identify factors that increase or decrease their risks. There are few certainties regarding cancer causation at the level of the individual person, but a great deal is known about the odds for larger populations of people. It is up to each person to use this information wisely.

## SUMMARY

Scientists use the tools of epidemiology and experimentation to determine the causes of cancer. Epidemiology helps us establish links between carcinogens and the cancers that develop. Experimentation provides confirmation about the biological mechanisms that account for the development of cancer. People can use the information gained from epidemiology and experimentation to minimize their own cancer risks.

# 3

## CANCER AND LIFESTYLE

---

**KEY POINTS**

♦ The majority of cancers are caused by factors we can control, such as smoking, poor diet, alcohol use, and lack of exercise.

♦ It is difficult to connect personal behaviors to the development of cancer because there is such a long time between exposure to a carcinogen and the formation of a tumor.

♦ Carcinogens cause cancer by damaging DNA in cells, thus producing mistakes in the inherited instructions.

---

According to epidemiological research, more than 80 percent of all cancers in the United States are due to extrinsic, or external, causes, including diet, personal habits, and environmental factors. In this chapter we will consider several major lifestyle choices that can influence cancer development: smoking, poor diet, alcohol use, and lack of exercise.

Given that many cancers are caused by identifiable, controllable factors, we might ask: Why don't people adjust their behaviors so that these cancers can be avoided? We have the amazing power to prevent the occurrence of most cancers, and yet it seems so difficult to do so. It can be hard for people to make the connection between their behaviors and the risk of developing cancer, or to have the discipline to stop risky behaviors. As discussed in the previous chapter, epidemiological research can identify a person's relative risk, but it cannot predict the specific outcome for an individual. It is easy to think "it won't happen to me." In addition the time between exposure to a carcinogen, such as tobacco smoke, and the development of a tumor can be decades. People do not often think about events that might not happen for 20 or more years. Finally many of the behaviors that can cause cancer are pleasurable and even addictive. It is not easy to change.

## TOBACCO

In 1948 Ernest Wynder was a young medical student who was studying at New York University for the summer. While there he observed the autopsy of a man who had had lung cancer. Wynder heard the man's widow say that her husband had smoked two packs of cigarettes a day for many years. Wynder wondered whether there might be a connection between the cigarettes and the man's lung cancer.

At the end of the summer Wynder returned to medical school at Washington University and approached Dr. Evarts Graham, a distinguished thoracic surgeon, to see if Graham would help him determine whether there was a link between cigarette smoking and lung cancer. Graham, a heavy smoker, was not convinced of the need for such a study, but he supported Wynder's efforts anyway. Wynder conducted a well-designed study, published in 1950, which dramatically demonstrated that the risk of lung cancer was 40 times greater for smokers

## SPOTLIGHT ON CANCER SCIENTISTS
### SIR RICHARD DOLL (1912–2005)

Richard Doll was born in 1912, the son of a general practitioner. Doll's father encouraged his son to go to medical school, but Doll was more interested in mathematics. Because the family did not have a lot of money, Doll tried to win a mathematics scholarship. He did wonderfully on the first three days of the qualifying tests. On the night before the last day of exams, however, some older students took him out for a night of beer drinking. The next day Doll was hung over and did not perform well. The university did not give him the scholarship. Doll was so upset with himself that he decided to follow his father's advice and go to medical school instead. He went to St. Thomas' Hospital to study medicine and never looked back.

**Figure 3.1** Sir Richard Doll. (*Damian Dovarganes, AP Images*)

By the early 1930s scientists were becoming alarmed by the ever-increasing rates of lung cancer mortality. Scientists first hypothesized that

than for nonsmokers. The data were so convincing that Graham, a lifelong smoker, quit smoking in 1951. Uunfortunately, he died of lung cancer in 1957.

---

the cause of lung cancer was tobacco, but when pathologists (scientists who specialize in disease) tested this idea by brushing tobacco onto the skin of mice, no cancer resulted and scientists concluded that tobacco did not cause cancer. Although lung cancer mortality continued to climb, the research was put on the back burner because of World War II.

By the time the war ended in 1945, lung cancer had become an even worse problem. At the same time that Ernst Wynder and Evarts Graham were performing their study on the association between lung cancer and cigarette smoking, Doll and his colleague Bradford Hill were doing a similar study in England.

Doll and Hill, then working at the London School of Hygiene, set out to determine the cause. They did a careful study that showed very clearly that the culprit behind the lung cancer epidemic was tobacco in general and cigarette smoking in particular. Doll stopped smoking as soon as he began to analyze the data. Doll and Hill published their work in late 1950, a few months after Wynder and Graham.

After his initial paper with Hill on the effects of smoking on lung cancer incidence, Doll extended his study of the effects of tobacco on human health by starting the Doctors Project, which is also known as the British Doctors' Study. He followed the smoking habits of 40,000 doctors for 50 years. The information gained from this recently completed study has demonstrated the association between smoking and other diseases besides cancer, as well as the effects of quitting smoking after having smoked for various lengths of time. Doll was knighted in 1971 for his work.

During the time that Wynder was doing his research, another study looking at smoking and lung cancer was being done in the United Kingdom. The results of this work were published six months after Wynder and Graham's paper, and the British researchers, Richard Doll and Bradford Hill, came to the same conclusion. It was clear by 1950 that smoking is a major cause of lung cancer, yet it was decades before this fact was acknowledged by most people. Some people still will not believe the danger of smoking, even though the United States and Western Europe are experiencing an epidemic of lung cancer that started in the first half of the twentieth century.

Why are people so resistant to the idea that smoking is harmful? Graham's words to Wynder upon viewing the final version of their paper capture some of the reason:

> You are going to have a great many difficulties. The smokers will not like your message. The tobacco interests will be vigorously opposed. The media and the government will be loath to support these findings. But you have one factor in your favor. What you have going for you is that you are right.[2]

How bad is the risk of cancer due to cigarette smoking and other types of tobacco use? Consider the following scenario: If you followed the lives of 1,000 young men who smoked their entire adult lives, on average one will be murdered, six will die in car accidents, and 250 will die of tobacco-related diseases, including cancer. Tobacco is implicated in several types of cancers. For example people who use snuff, a powdered form of tobacco that can be sniffed, suffer disproportionately from nasal cancers, whereas pipe smokers and people who chew tobacco are at an increased risk for oral cancers, such as those of the lips, tongue, or throat. For pipe smokers, the lower lip is particularly vulnerable. Cigarette smokers are more prone to lung cancer. In addition, cigarette smoking also increases the risk of cancers of the mouth, pharynx, larynx, pancreas, bladder, kidney, colon, and rectum. If a person starts smoking at a young age, the risk of cancer is even greater. Secondhand smoke kills as many people as exposure to **radon**, a radioactive gas, or air pollution.

If we consider the overall incidence of tobacco-related cancers and the mortality due to these cancers, the numbers are astonishing. Smoking is responsible for 80 to 90 percent of lung cancers and 30 percent of all cancer deaths. At present, two to four million people die each year worldwide because of tobacco, and 40 percent of these deaths are due to lung cancer. Although cigarette smoking is declining in some developed countries, such as the United States, the practice is very common in China, India, Eastern Europe, and Africa. In fact one-third of the world's smokers are Chinese. Epidemiologists estimate that more than 30 percent of Chinese men who now smoke will die of a tobacco-related illness by 2050; this translates into 10 million deaths. The estimated worldwide annual death rate due to tobacco will be 10 million people per year by 2030.

How does exposure to tobacco or tobacco smoke produce cancer? The probable explanation is that repeated exposure to the more than 40 carcinogens present in tobacco tar, a by-product of burning tobacco, damages cells in ways that turn normal cells into cancerous ones. Specifically the carcinogens in tobacco tar damage DNA. If the damaged DNA is in **genes** that are necessary for controlling normal cell division and behavior, cancer can result. Two of the most potent carcinogens found in tobacco tar—benzo(a)pyrene and nitrosamine—are found attached to the DNA in the lung cells of smokers. The metabolic breakdown

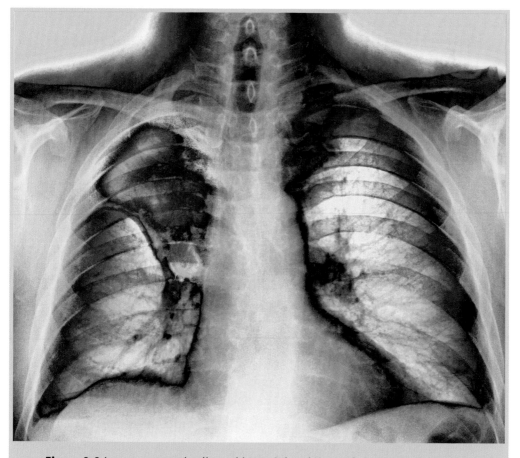

**Figure 3.2** Lung cancer and collapsed lung. Colored X-ray of the chest of a patient with a cancer in the right lung (at left). The cancer (pink/blue, round) is at center left. The cancer has caused the upper lobe of the right lung to collapse as shown by the curved red line to the left of the cancer. This line shows the upper boundary of the right lung, which is now greatly reduced in size compared to the left lung (at right). (*Du Cane Medical Imaging Ltd./Photo Researcher, Inc.*)

product of benzo(a)pyrene, has been shown experimentally to bind to a particular gene (named *p53*), which is known to be important in cancer development. The lung cells of smokers who do not have lung cancer also exhibit molecular and chromosomal damage in amounts proportional to how much and how long they have been smoking.

The relationship between tobacco use and cancer was suspected for hundreds of years and has been well documented for more than 50 years. Yet people continue to smoke and use other forms of tobacco, despite epidemiological research that quitting dramatically reduces the risk of developing cancers—sometimes bringing the risk down to the same levels as those seen in nonsmokers.

What events helped lead to the development of this smoking culture and the subsequent lung cancer epidemic? First, the 1880s saw the invention of cigarette-making machines. Cheap cigarettes became readily available to a large population. Second, cigarettes were provided free of charge to soldiers during World War I and World War II. In fact soldiers were encouraged to smoke in order to relax. The result of giving away cigarettes was the development of a large population of smokers who became role models for other people. Smoking became a common activity that spread throughout the wider population, and since tobacco contains nicotine, an addictive substance, quitting smoking is very difficult. Finally, tobacco products were marketed and sold without concern for the potentially deadly effects. Conditions were perfect for setting up the largest unintended experiment ever—namely, seeing the long-term effects of smoking on billions of people.

## DIET AND EXERCISE

Interestingly the types of cancers that people commonly develop vary quite a lot in different countries. For example cancer of the breast, prostate, colon, and rectum are more prevalent in affluent, developed nations such as the United States and in the countries of

Western Europe. In contrast, cancers commonly seen in developing areas such as parts of Asia and Africa are of the mouth, esophagus, stomach, liver, and **cervix**. One major reason for some of these differences appears to be the type of diet people eat. In fact smoking accounts for 30 percent of all cancer deaths in the United States, and diet accounts for another 35 percent. What features of diet affect the risk of developing cancer? In affluent countries, the culprits are too much saturated fat, too much red meat, inadequate amounts of fruits and vegetables, and insufficient amounts of fiber. A lack of exercise, particularly during the childhood and teen years, also plays a role, especially in the eventual development of breast and prostate cancers. Eating too much and exercising too little during childhood, which can lead to excessive early growth, build up of body fat, and early sexual maturation, are responsible for 5 percent of breast and prostate cancers in adults. Evidence that the Westernized diet is leading to an increased cancer risk comes from studies of immigrant health. For example the incidence of breast cancer is very low in Japanese women. However in one generation after immigration to the United States, Japanese-American women's rate of breast cancer is the same rate as the rate in American women whose families have been living in the United States for many generations.

Let's look more closely at the Western diet and why it increases the risk of cancer. Thousands of years ago, our human ancestors probably got 66 percent of their calories from fruits and vegetables and 33 percent from lean meats. Perhaps they also supplemented this diet with eggs and fish. In contrast average Americans today consume 50 percent of their calories in the forms of cereal, milk, dairy products, refined foods, and sweets; 17 percent from fruits and vegetables; and 28 percent from domesticated (farm-raised) meat, not lean wild animals. Our human ancestors also engaged in a great deal more physical activity than the average person does today.

The consequences of our modern diet are clear. The incidences of cancer of the colon and rectum are 10 times higher in the United States, Canada, Western Europe, and New Zealand than in other places around the world. It is also evident that changing the diet can lower a person's risk for cancer. Regularly eating fresh fruits and vegetables lowers cancer risk. The relative percentage of fruits and vegetables in our diets should probably be more similar to what our ancestors ate.

Why do fruits and vegetables lower the risk of cancer? First, plants contain vitamins and minerals, some of which help the functioning of enzymes that repair DNA damage. Second, along with vitamins and minerals, other plant chemicals, called **flavanoids**, prevent DNA damage and loss of function. Finally, the large amount of fiber found in fruits and vegetables probably helps lower cancer risk by neutralizing bile acids and other potentially harmful chemicals, and by scouring the large intestine, thus removing materials that might damage the cells that line the colon and rectum.

Although the colon and rectum are potential trouble spots for cancer among Americans and Western Europeans, this has not always been the case. Once common throughout Europe, stomach cancer killed more Americans in 1900 than any other type of cancer (lung cancer was still rare at that time). During the twentieth century, the incidence of stomach cancer declined dramatically. Since 1945 stomach cancer incidence has declined five-fold. However, this disease continues to occur frequently in Japan. Why? What changed in the United States but not in Japan?

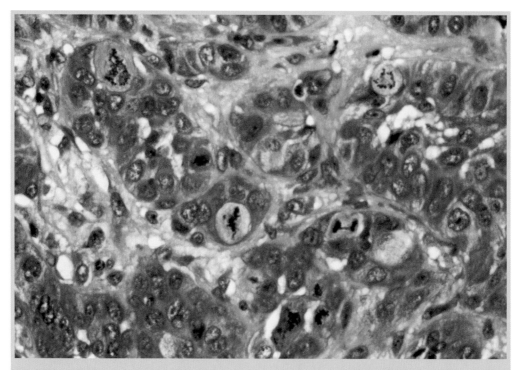

**Figure 3.3** Stomach cancer. Light micrograph of a section through an adeno-carcinoma in stomach tissue. Stomach cancer is one of the leading causes of cancer deaths. (*CNRI/Photo Researchers, Inc.*)

Stomach cancer is linked to the use of salt as a food preservative. Refrigeration and other types of food preservation were developed in the twentieth century. For Americans, these innovations cut down on salt consumption. However, stomach cancer is also linked to eating pickled foods of many kinds that are popular in Japan. It is probably this dietary practice that continues to be the cause of stomach cancer in Japan.

## ALCOHOL

Of the items we choose to take into our bodies by inhalation or ingestion, tobacco and food account for at least two-thirds of all human cancers. By this measure, alcohol plays a less significant role as a risk factor for cancer. Nevertheless it is an important element in the causal network of carcinogenesis, being responsible for three percent of all cancers.

Alcohol use is linked to increased incidences of a few specific cancers, such as esophageal cancer, especially in smokers, probably because their esophagus is already irritated by exposure to tobacco smoke. Similarly, drinkers who smoke also experience higher incidences of cancers of the upper respiratory tract and liver. Alcohol is also implicated in breast cancer. Even one drink per day can increase the risk of breast cancer by approximately 10 percent. Although scientists are not sure of the mechanism, alcohol does not appear to be directly carcinogenic for breast tissue. Instead, alcohol may exert its effect by interacting with the important nutrient folate. Alcohol binds to folate, decreasing the amount in the blood. Since folate is important for DNA repair, alcohol may be influencing the development of breast cancer by reducing or preventing the repair of mutated or damaged DNA in cells. As with tobacco and diet, with alcohol there is a relationship between DNA damage and the development of cancer.

## SUMMARY

Most cancers in the United States are caused by smoking, eating a poor diet, and not getting enough exercise, particularly during youth.

Although it may be difficult to do, changing risky behaviors could prevent cancer. Carcinogens all operate by damaging DNA in some manner, resulting in the transformation of a normal cell to a cancerous one. Since the transformation process can take place over a long time, adopting healthy behaviors at any time may help reduce cancer risk.

# 4

# INFECTIOUS AGENTS
# AS CAUSES OF CANCER

---

**KEY POINTS**

◆ Some cancers are caused by infections by viruses, bacteria, or parasites.

◆ Approximately 15 to 20 percent of cancers worldwide are due to infections by viruses, bacteria, or parasites.

◆ Infectious causation of cancer is more common in developing parts of the world than in affluent developed countries.

◆ Infectious agents alone are generally not sufficient to cause cancer.

---

## DISCOVERY OF TUMOR VIRUSES: A LESSON FROM CHICKENS

In 1909 a farmer from Long Island, New York, made the trip into New York City to see Dr. Peyton Rous, a cancer researcher at the Rockefeller

Institute (now Rockefeller University). This farmer was on an important mission—one of his prize Plymouth Rock hens had a tumor in her right breast muscle. This farmer hoped that Rous could cure the bird. No one is exactly sure what happened next, but evidently Rous was very persuasive because he somehow managed to keep the chicken for further study.

Rous did two experiments that changed our understanding of cancer and paved the way for the research being done today. First, he removed the tumor from the chicken and transplanted it to another

---

## SPOTLIGHT ON CANCER SCIENTISTS
### PEYTON ROUS (1879–1970)

Born in Texas in 1879, Peyton Rous grew up in Baltimore, Maryland, where he earned his college and medical degrees from Johns Hopkins University. Rous deemed himself "unfit to be a 'real' doctor" and turned his attention instead to medical research. After a brief time working at the University of Michigan, Rous joined the Rockefeller Institute in 1909. He remained there conducting research until he was 90 years old. Despite his monumental discovery of a tumor virus a few years earlier, in 1915 Rous abandoned his work with tumors and turned his attention to liver physiology and blood. Along with J.R. Turner and O.H. Robertson, Rous pioneered methods for the safe and efficient handling and transfusion of blood. This work led to the establishment of the world's first blood bank in 1917, during World War I. Rous ultimately returned to cancer research in 1934. He collaborated

chicken from the farmer's flock. The chicken that received the transplant developed cancer, which showed that cancer could be transferred from one organism to another. In his next experiment, Rous ground up tumor tissue, collected extract or the liquid that was squeezed out of the tissue, filtered the extract so that no cells were present in it, and injected the **filtrate** into another chicken. The injected chicken developed tumors. This experiment showed that some infectious agent—we now know it was a **virus**—caused cancer. Viruses are parasites that are too small to be seen with a **light microscope**. Ironically, Rous

with Richard Shope on the study of a virus that caused giant warts in rabbits. Sometimes these warts became malignancies. This research was very important because it showed that some mammalian cancers could be caused by viruses. Cancer-causing viruses were not limited to birds.

Rous was 87 years old when he was awarded the Nobel Prize. The 55-year interval between Rous's discovery of a tumor-causing virus in 1911 and his receipt of the Nobel Prize in Physiology or Medicine in 1966 is certainly an example of delayed recognition.

**Figure 4.1** Peyton Rous. (*National Institutes of Health/U.S. National Library of Medicine.*)

stopped this particular avenue of research because he was unable to demonstrate the viral induction of cancer in mammals and thought (incorrectly) that this phenomenon was limited to chickens and not of larger significance. During the early twentieth century most scientists and physicians just did not believe that it was possible that a virus could cause cancer.

## INFECTIOUS AGENTS AND CANCER

It turns out that those scientists and physicians who thought viruses could not cause cancer were wrong. Despite the prevailing view that viral infection was unrelated to carcinogenesis, some scientists did continue to study the problem. In the 1930s two cancer viruses were discovered in mammals. One, isolated by the Rockefeller Institute scientist Richard Shope, produced cancer in rabbits; another, studied by John Bittner, a scientist at the Jackson Lab, caused a mouse mammary tumor that could be transmitted through milk.

After the description of the structure of DNA in 1953 and the visualization of viruses in 1957 by **electron microscopy**, biomedical researchers became a lot more interested in studying the infectious origins of cancer. In the 1960s two human cancer viruses—hepatitis B virus and Epstein-Barr virus—were discovered. Then, in the late 1960s, the U.S. Virus Cancer Program was initiated. This research effort has revealed that many types of cancer are associated with infection by specific viruses, bacteria, and other parasites. In fact approximately 15 to 20 percent of the world's cancer deaths are due to infection. The actual percentage varies depending on the particular country. In the United States, for example, approximately 5 percent of cancer fatalities are due to infection. In contrast, cancer mortality due to infection exceeds 20 percent in many developing nations. The

## SPOTLIGHT ON CANCER SCIENTISTS
### JOHN BITTNER (1904–1961)

The medical community in the first half of the twentieth century was very resistant to the idea that a virus—or any infectious agent—could cause cancer. In 1936 Dr. John Bittner, then working at the Jackson Laboratory in Bar Harbor, Maine, published a paper in *Science* in which he described the transmission of a factor in mother's milk that could cause mammary cancer in mice. For years, Bittner had studied this phenomenon and thought he had evidence that the factor was a virus. Even so, he continued to use the term *milk factor* to describe it in his publications and grant proposals. Years later Bittner was asked why he initially hid his discovery of an **oncogenic** virus. He explained, "If I had called it a virus, my grant applications would have automatically been put in the category of 'unacceptable proposals.' As long as I used the word *factor*, it was respectable genetics." Bittner also hid his suspicions about the viral nature of his factor because he did not want to irritate his supervisor, Clarence Cook Little, who controlled Bittner's research support and also thought the viral induction of cancer was nonsense. Eventually the scientific research community recognized that viruses can indeed cause some cancers. Today the factor in mouse milk is called Bittner's virus.

global death toll from cancer due to infection is approximately 1.2 million people per year.

There are several ways that infection can produce cancer. First, many viruses, bacteria, and parasites produce chronic inflammation in the affected tissues. Inflammation is a response to tissue or cellular injury in which tissues swell, leak fluids, and become warm, red, and ir-ritated. As a result of this response, cells, proteins, cell membranes, and DNA can be damaged. If any of this damage occurs in the genes or cell structures that control cell proliferation, tumors can form. In addition some infectious agents disrupt genes that are important for preventing cancer. For example if a virus damages the DNA of a gene whose job is to stop cancer cells from growing uncontrollably, the infected cells can produce a tumor. In some cases infections can inhibit the normal immune response, reducing the immunosurveillance that normally prevents tumors from forming.

Even though the infectious agents that are associated with cancer are very prevalent, the development of cancer after exposure to these agents takes a long time. In fact these cancers are relatively rare and not everyone who is infected with a potential cancer-causing agent develops cancer. Like many other causes of cancer, infectious agents alone are generally not enough to produce cancer. Other factors—such as a person's health, whether the person survives the infection, lifestyle, socioeconomic status, gender, and certain environmental factors—also play roles in whether an infection will eventually cause a malignancy.

## WHICH SPECIFIC CANCERS ARE CAUSED BY INFECTION?

Epidemiological studies and laboratory research have revealed that several types of cancer are caused by specific viruses. Two of the most common oncogenic, or cancer-causing, viruses are the human papil-lomavirus (HPV) and the hepatitis B virus (HBV). The human papil-lomavirus is responsible for 70 to 80 percent of the world's cancer of the genitals and anus, while HBV and the similarly named but different

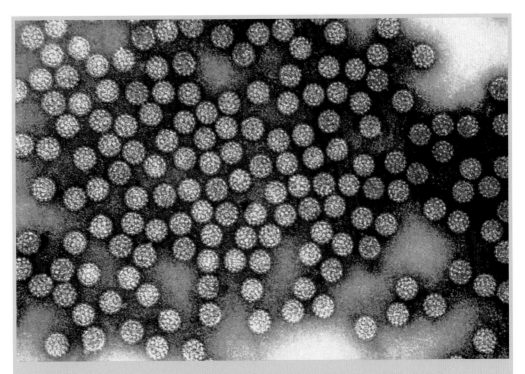

**Figure 4.2** Color-enhanced transmission electron microscopy (magnification = 27,000x) of negatively stained human papillomavirus (HPV), isolated from common warts. (*Kwangshin Kim/Photo Researchers, Inc.*)

hepatitis C virus (HCV), account for 80 percent of the liver cancer cases in the world. Let's look more closely at HPV and HBV, two important **pathogens**, or disease-causing agents.

The human papillomavirus (HPV) spreads from person to person by sexual contact. The prevalence of the virus is lowest among nuns and sexually inexperienced individuals. The virus is much more commonly present among sexually active people. The number of sexual partners determines the level of risk, as does the age at which the person first engaged in sexual activity. The more partners and the earlier sexual activity begins, the greater the risk of infection. Interestingly there is a strong relationship between the likelihood of infection and a couple in a marriage or committed relationship: If one partner is infected, the other one is at a higher risk. As is the case with infectious disease in general, the prevalence of HPV is higher in developing nations (15 percent) than in developed ones (7 percent). The specific cancers caused by HPV include those of the vulva, anus, penis, and especially the cervix. HPV is responsible for 80 to 90 percent of cervical cancer cases worldwide. The second most common cancer affecting women in the world, cervical cancer, is rare in the United States and many other developed countries because women are able to get **Pap tests** to screen for this disease. Pap tests can detect precancerous changes in the cervix at a very early stage. Consequently treatment can be implemented before the cancer becomes unmanageable.

Like HPV, HBV can be transmitted sexually. HBV can also be spread **perinatally** (from mother to child), during childhood (between siblings, for example), and at any age by transfusion of infected blood or intravenous drug use. The number of people infected with HBV is enormous—2 billion worldwide. Of these, 350 million people are chronically infected carriers, meaning that while they may not feel sick, they carry the virus and can infect others. Once again developing nations are hardest hit—China, other parts of Asia, and Africa have the world's highest prevalence of HBV infection. HBV produces chronic inflammation in the liver. The resulting cellular and DNA damage set the stage for the development of liver tumors.

In addition to the human papillomavirus and hepatitis B and C viruses, several other viruses have been linked to specific cancers. The Epstein-Barr virus (EBV) infects more than 90 percent of the

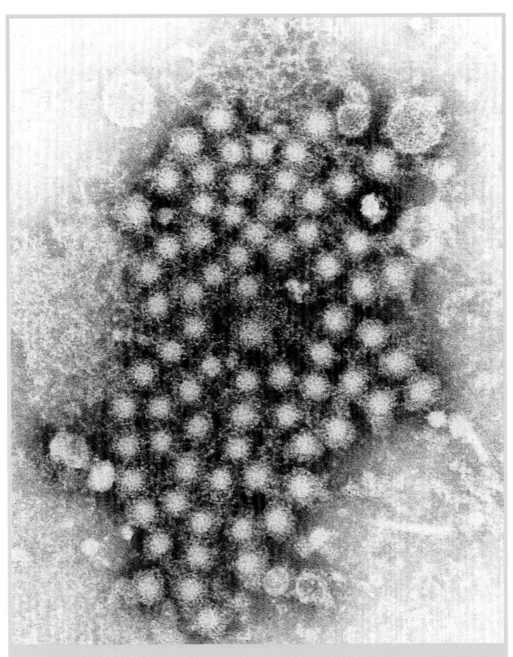

**Figure 4.3** This transmission electron micrograph (TEM) revealed numerous hepatitis virions (virus particles) of an unknown strain of the organism. *(CDC)*

world's population. For most people the infection is benign and can even go unnoticed. For others—particularly young adults in developed nations—EBV causes **mononucleosis**, a temporary, noncancerous infection of the **lymph** tissue, which is a part of the immune system. In developing nations, however, infection with EBV sometimes leads to various types of **lymphoma**, such as Hodgkin's disease, non-Hodgkin's lymphoma, or Burkitt's lymphoma. Lymphoma is a malignancy that involves the enlargement of the lymph nodes, spleen, and liver. EBV can also sometimes cause **nasopharyngeal** cancer, meaning that tumors form in the nasal passages and pharynx.

Other examples of human oncogenic viruses include the human herpes virus 8 (HHV-8), which causes Kaposi's **sarcoma**, a malignancy that produces red or purple blotches especially on the lower extremities; and non-Hodgkin's lymphoma. Another oncogenic virus is the human thymus-derived-cell **leukemia**/lymphoma virus-1 (HTLV-1), which causes adult T-cell leukemia, which is a malignancy of certain cells of the immune system. The human immunodeficiency virus (HIV, or the AIDS virus) is another oncogenic virus. It causes Kaposi's sarcoma and non-Hodgkin's lymphoma.

Viruses are by no means the only infectious agents that are capable of causing cancer. The bacterium *Helicobacter pylorus* (abbreviated *H. pylori*) is a known carcinogen, and there may be other bacterial causes of cancer. Causing persistent, chronic bacterial infections of the stomach, *H. pylori* is linked to stomach cancer, the second most common malignancy worldwide. In 1998, stomach cancer killed 800,000 people. As we saw in Chapter 3, stomach cancer was once the most prevalent cause of cancer mortality in the United States, although today it is rare. In contrast, stomach cancer incidences continue to be very high in eastern Asia, Central America, tropical South America, and Eastern Europe.

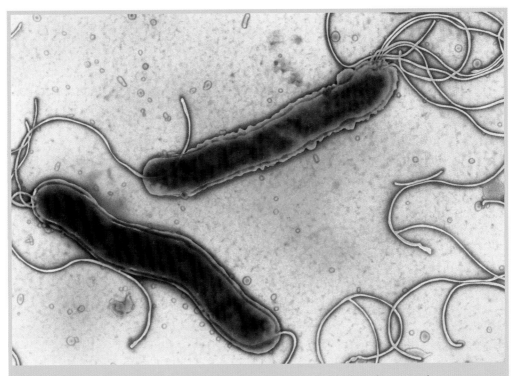

**Figure 4.4** *Helicobacter pylori* bacteria. Colored transmission electron micrograph (TEM) of a section through *Helicobacter pylori* bacteria. (*NIBSC/Photo Resarchers, Inc.*)

Why is there so much more stomach cancer in these places than in the United States? Some, but not all, of the differences can be attributed to cultural and dietary practices. However, a big part of the story is the relative prevalence of *H. pylori* in the population. In the United States, for example, scientists have shown that as *H. pylori* infection decreased in the population, probably due to improved water quality, the incidence of stomach cancer also decreased. In contrast, stomach cancer is still widespread in Japan, where the incidence of *H. pylori* infection is 80 percent.

As we have seen with several other carcinogens (including salt, pickling brine, and viruses), *H. pylori* probably causes cancer because it produces chronic inflammation, which leads to cellular and DNA damage.

Besides viruses and bacteria, there are actually some parasitic worms that can cause cancer. **Schistosomes** are parasitic blood flukes, or flatworms, that infect 200 million people worldwide. These worms cause bladder cancer in some of those infected. Another type of flatworm, the liver fluke, can cause liver cancer. Infection with both parasites and the corresponding cancers are more prevalent in developing countries than in affluent areas. In both cases, cancer probably occurs because the parasites trigger chronic inflammatory responses.

## WHY DOES INFECTION AS A CAUSE OF CANCER VARY GLOBALLY?

People infected with oncogenic pathogens do not all get cancer. Why is this? Can the question be answered by simply looking at the specific characteristics of individuals, or must we consider cultural, political, economic, and social factors as well? It is clear that personal habits, general health, **genetic background**, and living conditions affect how well the immune system and other body systems operate. If the functioning of the body is compromised for any reason, the risk of chronic infection increases. Even so, comparisons of rates of infection and incidences of cancers caused by infection clearly show that socioeconomic status matters. As we have already discussed, the prevalence of cancer caused by HPV, HBV, EBV, *H. pylori*, and parasitic flukes is higher in developing regions than in affluent places.

One could argue that poverty is itself a significant risk factor for cancer. Poor people often have inadequate nutrition, greater exposure to infectious agents, and limited access to health care. When an entire nation is poor, this poverty is reflected in patterns of disease, including cancer.

## SUMMARY

Infectious agents are a major cause of cancer worldwide, but particularly in developing nations. Infections probably cause cancer by producing chronic inflammation that ultimately results in DNA damage. It is likely that infection with carcinogenic viruses, bacteria, or parasites will not cause cancer by itself. Other factors, including overall health, are important, too.

# 5

# RADIATION AND CANCER

---

**KEY POINTS**

♦ Some forms of radiation, such as ultraviolet light, X rays, and gamma rays, can cause cancer.

♦ High-energy radiation causes cancer by damaging DNA.

♦ Low-energy forms of radiation, such as those emanating from electrical power stations, cell phones, and radio or television antennae, have not been convincingly associated with cancer.

---

## DEADLY MINES

People have mined for silver in the Ore Mountains near Schneeberg and Jachymov, Czech Republic, since 1470. Within decades the local people noticed that many miners were afflicted with a terrible lung disease. Because the incidence of this disease was so particular to miners in the region, the sickness was referred to as Schneeberg lung disease. During the seventeenth and eighteenth centuries, the Ore Mountain mines prospered economically, thanks to an increase in silver mining and also because both cobalt and copper were being mined, too. Unfortunately this mining boom was accompanied by an increase in the incidence of Schneeberg lung disease. In the 1870s two local physicians, Dr. Hesse and Dr. Harting, recognized that this disease was actually lung cancer. They estimated that 75 percent of all former miners had died from this disease.

What was causing this cancer? The miners themselves realized that working in the mines was dangerous to their health. They even had a sense of the relative dangers of specific mines. In 1913 H.E. Muller, a reformer who worked for the benefit of miners, discovered the mines were causing cancer because they were **radioactive**, which meant that they contained elements whose atoms could give off particles and very high-energy waves in the form of **radiation**. In fact the mines of the Ore Mountains are rich with radioactive materials, including radium. The mines also produced the radioactive gas radon, which was inhaled by miners and eventually caused their lung cancers. Interestingly, when technology improved so that levels of radon could be measured, it turned out that the area the miners called the "death mine" did in fact have the highest levels of radon.

Even though there was clear evidence that radon gas and other sources of radioactivity could be deadly for miners, work continued in mines all over the world. Miners generally used little or no protective gear. In the 1940s, during World War II, mining for the radioactive element uranium began in earnest because of its potential military use in the development of atomic bombs. One of the natural products of uranium's decay is none other than radon. It should come as no surprise that studies done in the 1950s and 1960s showed unequivocally that the risk of lung cancer was dramatically increased among miners because of their exposure to radon. It has been estimated that at least 500,000 people worked in uranium mines during the 1940s and 1950s. Thousands died from lung cancer as a result.

## WHY DOES RADIATION CAUSE CANCER?

Electromagnetic energy travels through space in waves of various energy levels. We are most directly familiar with electromagnetic energy, or radiation, in the form of visible light. In addition to visible light, we are exposed to other forms of radiation. Some of these types of radiation have more energy than visible light, whereas others have less. For instance **ultraviolet (UV) light** has more energy than visible light, X rays have even more energy, and **gamma rays**—the type of radiation given off by many radioactive materials—are even more energetic. Types of radiation that have lower energy than visible light include radio waves and microwaves.

Radiation from all possible sources is responsible for approximately two percent of all cancer deaths. Many possible radiation risks have been proposed, including radon; radiation from nuclear power plants; X rays; electrical and magnetic fields generated by power lines; cell phones; antennae used for radios, televisions, and cell phones; household appliances; and the sun.

In addition to identifying possible associations between exposure to a potential carcinogen such as radiation and the development of cancer, it is important to determine a biologically plausible mechanism to account for the formation of a tumor. With respect to the relationship between X rays and cancer, the first experimental evidence came from a study done by French physician Jean Clunet in 1908. Clunet exposed four rats to an intensive beam of X rays. Two rats died and two survived.

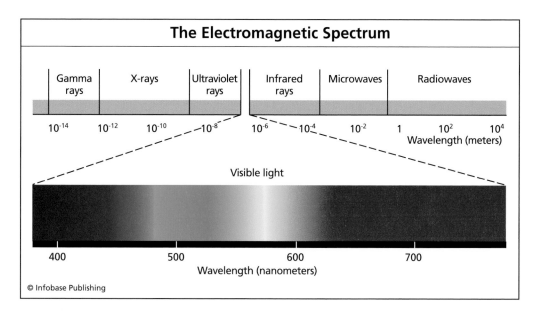

**Figure 5.1** The electromagnetic spectrum.

One of the survivors developed a tumor at the site of irradiation. With this simple experiment, Clunet showed that cancer could be induced experimentally by X rays.

A clue regarding why X rays could cause cancer came from a completely different avenue of research. In 1928, American geneticist Hermann J. Muller bombarded *Drosophila melanogaster*, the common fruit fly, with X rays. Muller was able to show that X rays could induce mutations. Therefore X rays were both **mutagenic** *and* carcinogenic. Evidently X rays can damage DNA and, in some cells of certain organisms, this damage can lead to cellular changes that result in cancer. X rays are able to damage DNA because they can directly remove **electrons** and, thus, **ionize** molecules. In all cases where radiation has been found to cause cancer, it has also been shown that DNA function or structure, or both, have been damaged.

## SPOTLIGHT ON CANCER SCIENTISTS
### JEAN CLUNET (1878–1917)

Jean Clunet was born in Paris in 1878 and received his medical education there. He joined the Medical Corps of the French Army, serving as a major. Clunet was on active duty and had frequent brushes with death, both from warfare and disease. While serving in Morocco in 1914, Clunet and other French soldiers were surrounded and threatened with execution. They escaped, but Clunet contracted **dysentery**. He served during World War I and, although he was not injured in battle, he was infected with **dengue fever**. In 1916, Clunet was sent to the Middle East on a military transport ship. An enemy submarine sank the ship, but Clunet survived and directed the rescue operations and emergency medical care for the other soldiers involved. After this close call, Clunet went to Romania to set up a military hospital. By this point his luck had run out. Clunet contracted **typhus**, probably from a patient, and died in 1917. Clunet had certainly lived a life fraught with peril as he worked to help others. His work did provide important contributions, however.

After the discovery of X rays in 1895, it quickly became clear that they had important applications for both medical diagnosis and therapy. Within a short while it also became evident that X rays could be hazardous. Radiological technicians who used X rays regularly frequently developed dermatitis, skin ulcers, and, in some cases, metastatic cancers. Scientists hypothesized that X ray exposure was the cause of these cancers. When Jean Clunet did his experiment in 1908 in which he exposed rats to X rays, he was trying to reproduce a clinical observation in a laboratory experiment. His success was important because he provided a way to figure out what specific events might lead to cancer in people exposed to excessive radiation.

## "ACCIDENTAL EXPERIMENTS" THAT VERIFIED THE CARCINOGENIC EFFECTS OF HIGH-ENERGY RADIATION

In addition to the exposure of uranium miners to radon and other radioactive materials, other groups of people have experienced long-term exposure to radiation for various reasons. The information gathered about these individuals has strengthened the case for a causal role for high-energy, or ionizing, radiation in cancer development. One of the biggest "experiments" was the exposure of the populations of Hiroshima and Nagasaki, Japan, to the fallout from the U.S. detonations of atomic bombs in 1945. The health of the atomic blast survivors has been monitored for decades. These studies have revealed higher incidences of breast cancer in both men and women, thyroid cancer, and leukemia. The relative risks of developing these cancers were proportional to the dose of radiation experienced by the individuals.

In some cases radiation exposure occurred because of good intentions, namely medical treatment. From the 1930s through the 1950s, before people fully understood the potential dangers, radiation was used for a variety of therapeutic reasons, and some people developed cancer as a result. For example women treated with broad field X rays for Hodgkin's disease had a dramatically increased risk for breast cancer. Girls who were treated between the ages of 13 and 16 years had a breast cancer risk of 40 percent. Females exposed to X rays as a treatment for ringworm also showed an increased risk for both breast cancer and leukemia. Women treated for **tuberculosis** by **fluoroscopy** have an increased incidence of breast cancer. Radiation treatments for ankylosing spondylitis (an arthritic condition) and noncancerous gynecological conditions also increased the incidence of leukemia. Perhaps the saddest example of all: X rays used for routine pelvic exams during pregnancy caused a 40 percent increase in childhood leukemia.

## SPOTLIGHT ON CANCER SCIENTISTS
### HERMANN JOSEPH MULLER (1890–1967)

As the first person to purposely induce mutations in genes, Hermann J. Muller made an important contribution to cancer research, even though that had not been his intention. In fact Muller was more interested in gene structure and function and evolution. His research organism, the fruit fly (*Drosophila melanogaster*), had never been used to study cancer or any other human disease. Muller's breakthrough is a good example of how discoveries in one area of science—in this case, genetics—can have an enormous impact on another area.

Hermann J. Muller was born in New York City in 1890. He received his education in public schools and attended Columbia University as both an undergraduate and graduate student. Muller did his graduate work under the guidance of the Nobel laureate T.H. Morgan, the man responsible for first using *Drosophila* as a genetic tool. After he earned his Ph.D., Muller held a variety of professional positions. Ultimately he became a professor at the University of Texas–Austin in 1920. It was there that Muller did his experiments with x-ray-induced mutations that won him the Nobel Prize in Physiology or Medicine in 1946.

Before winning the Nobel Prize, Muller suffered an emotional breakdown in 1931 and tried to commit suicide, despairing because of his failed marriage, concerns about competition with his mentor, T.H. Morgan, and discomfort with the political environment in Texas. Fortunately Muller's colleagues intervened and saved him. Muller recovered and then traveled,

**Figure 5.2**  Nobel prize-winner professor Hermann Muller shows tubes with fruit flies to fellow Nobel prize-winner professor James B. Sumner in Sweden on December 12, 1946. Professor Muller brought the tubes with him from Indiana. (*AP Images*)

researching and teaching. He lived and worked in Germany, Russia, and Scotland, and eventually returned to the United States. In 1945 Muller accepted a position at Indiana University and resumed his research on radiation-induced mutation. He was an early voice warning about the human health dangers of excessive radiation exposure.

Scientists eventually recognized the risks associated with radiation. Although X rays continue to be used for diagnostic purposes, they are much safer today because patients are properly shielded during their use. Although radon continues to be a safety concern in mines and even in homes in some areas where it seeps out of the ground and collects in basements, the danger is very much reduced because radon can be monitored and eliminated with proper ventilation. Many people also express concern about the safety of working at or near a nuclear power plant. Despite these worries, studies have not revealed a clear increased risk for cancer due to exposure to radioactive discharges from local nuclear facilities. There are also no increases in the incidence of leukemia in people who live near nuclear power plants or in the children of nuclear reactor workers. In fact, in the case of the well-analyzed nuclear reactor accident at Chernobyl, Russia, where an explosion released large amounts of radioactive cesium and iodine, there was no increase in the incidence of childhood leukemia in the fallout area. Because iodine localizes in the thyroid gland normally, there was a significant increase in thyroid cancer among young people who had inhaled radioactive iodine that became concentrated in this organ. There were not, however, increases in any other type of childhood or adult cancers.

Although high-energy radiation in the form of X rays or gamma rays from radioactive materials probably doesn't constitute a large cancer risk for the general population, these kinds of radiation do present some risk to a particular group—those who receive radiation therapy for cancer. Approximately 1 to 5 percent of patients who are treated with radiation for leukemia, Hodgkin's disease, or ovarian cancer develop secondary leukemia because of the radiation therapy. Evidently the radiation cannot specifically target only the cancerous tissue. Instead it sometimes damages DNA in the normal cells, resulting in cancer.

## ULTRAVIOLET (UV) LIGHT AND SKIN CANCER

Even though many people are concerned and even frightened by the association between radiation and cancer, the majority of malignancies caused by radiation are actually preventable. All you have to do is avoid excess exposure to sunlight. Exposure to the UV rays present in sunlight is responsible for more than 90 percent of all skin cancers.

The rates of skin cancer are increasing dramatically worldwide. In the United States there are more than one million new cases reported each year. Most of these cancers are **basal cell carcinomas**, a less serious form of skin cancer that rarely metastasizes, and **squamous cell**

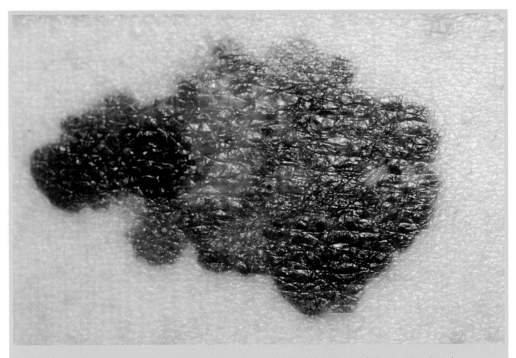

**Figure 5.3** Melanoma. (*National Institutes of Health/National Cancer Institute*)

**carcinoma**, which is more likely to spread. Of the one million annual cases, more than 50,000 will be **melanoma**, a highly aggressive, meta-static cancer. Of the 50,000 people diagnosed with melanoma, 7,000 will die of the disease.

Sunlight causes skin cancer because the sun emits UV light. There are three forms of UV light: A, B, and C. UV-C has the highest energy and is ordinarily absorbed by the ozone layer that surrounds the Earth. However if UV-C reaches the Earth, through an area of thinning or absent ozone, it will be absorbed by people's skin, which can directly produce DNA damage leading to cancer. UV-B has the next highest energy. It reaches the Earth's surface and is absorbed by exposed skin. Because UV-B has relatively high energy, it is able to damage DNA and cause mutations, some of which can lead to cancer. UV-A is also absorbed by the skin. Although its energy level is too low to damage DNA directly, it can still cause indirect damage by generating other reactive molecules, called **free radicals**, which can harm DNA. Excess UV from any source, whether the sun or tanning lights, increases the risk of developing skin cancer.

The dramatic increase in the incidence of all types of skin cancer is of great concern, but particularly worrisome is the increase in the number of cases of the most deadly form of skin cancer: melanoma. The incidence of melanoma has been rising since 1930 (when data were first collected). The current rates are 10 times higher than those of 50 years ago. Although most skin cancers are evident in people older than 50, melanoma is now a leading type of cancer among young adults.

All people have some chance of getting skin cancer from UV expo-sure. There are, however, some factors that are known to elevate the risk. For example, people who are redheaded, of fair complexion, sunburn easily and don't tan are at greatest risk. People are also more likely to be exposed to UV light if they live in a sunny and warm climate. For instance, the northeast coast of Australia (Queensland) is a particularly UV-rich environment. Early excessive exposure to UV also increases a person's later risk of cancer. The role of early UV exposure is evident in studies of people who immigrated to Australia. For those who immigrated at a young age, the risk of skin cancer was significantly higher than it was for those who immigrated at the age of 18 or older. Evidently UV damage to DNA during childhood was more likely to lead to changes that resulted in skin cancer.

## OTHER FORMS OF ELECTROMAGNETIC RADIATION

In addition to the high-energy radiation of UV light, X rays, and gamma rays, there are also low-energy forms of electromagnetic energy. Extremely low frequency (ELF) fields are those produced by electrical power stations and by the electricity in buildings. The energy level of these fields is too low to ionize molecules. Therefore they cannot damage DNA directly. Despite the public concerns, there is no evidence to link these kinds of fields with an increase in cancer.

Radio-frequency electromagnetic radiation is more energetic than ELF fields, but not powerful enough to ionize molecules. Radio-frequency radiation is emitted by cell phones, pagers, radio and television antennae, microwaves, wireless systems, and even living organisms. So far no one has found evidence to link this type of radiation with an increase in cancer incidence. Some people argue that it may be too early to rule out electromagnetic fields as a *possible* carcinogen because some technologies that emit this kind of energy, such as cell phones, have not been in widespread use for very long. Since there is often a long time lag, sometimes decades, between exposure to a carcinogen and the development of cancer, it may be too soon to assess the carcinogenicity of certain sources of electromagnetic radiation. Other people maintain that electromagnetic radiation in general, including that from cell phones, is simply not energetic enough to ionize molecules and damage DNA. Consequently this form of radiation cannot cause cancer by any cellular or molecular mechanism presently understood. Research in this area continues, spurred on by public concern.

## SUMMARY

Some, but not all, forms of radiation are carcinogenic. The most common cancer-causing radiation is ultraviolet (UV) light. Exposure to excessive sunlight is responsible for most skin cancers. Ionizing radiations, such as X rays or gamma rays, are also potent carcinogens. The forms of radiation that cause cancer are those that damage DNA in some way. Types of radiation that do not damage DNA, such as extremely low frequency and radio-frequency forms, have not been shown to cause cancer.

# 6

## OCCUPATIONAL AND ENVIRONMENTAL CARCINOGENS

---

**KEY POINTS**

♦ Cancers are caused by exposure to carcinogens in the workplace, at home, or in the environment.

♦ Air, water, and soil pollution are primarily responsible for 2 percent of cancer deaths in the United States.

♦ Less than 1 percent of cancer deaths in the United States can be attributed to pesticide exposure.

♦ Individuals have different responses to carcinogen exposure.

---

Examination of ancient human remains has revealed that cancer is an ancient disease. Not exclusive to humans, cancer is found in organisms of all vertebrate groups: fish, amphibians, reptiles, birds, and mammals.

In fact cancer has probably been around for at least 500 million years. Even though cancer has been a potentially deadly disease for humans since their origins, some aspects of modern life have had an impact on the prevalence of cancer.

# OCCUPATIONAL CANCERS

During the Industrial Revolution of the nineteenth century, workers were exposed to large amounts of chemicals and other substances. By the end of the nineteenth century, people suspected that some of these materials were harmful to workers' health and, in some cases, caused cancer. For example, paraffin oils, mining dust, arsenic dyes, and asbestos were all thought to be linked to the development of certain types of cancers. It was especially evident that factory workers who were continually exposed to oils and tars eventually got cancer on their exposed skin.

These were not the only cases of occupationally related cancers. As mentioned in earlier chapters, chimney sweeps experienced a higher incidence of scrotal cancer and miners who were exposed to radon and other radioactive materials developed lung cancer. The World Health Organization's International Agency for Research in Cancer (IARC) has identified more than 40 hazardous materials in the workplace that are associated with increases in particular cancers. Some of these chemicals that are known to be cancer-causing agents include asbestos, benzene, vinyl chloride, certain aromatic amines, formaldehyde, and diesel exhaust.

Scientists have been able to identify these occupational carcinogens because of unfortunate "natural experiments" in which workers were exposed to very high quantities of potentially hazardous substances. In 1950, before people realized the dangers, occupational exposure to carcinogenic chemicals accounted for approximately 10 percent of all cancer deaths. Today, with stricter regulations, this number has been cut in half, to approximately five percent. Unfortunately these safety improvements tend to be specific to developed nations. In developing areas of the world, the rapid industrialization that is still under way is probably going to result in an increase in occupational cancers.

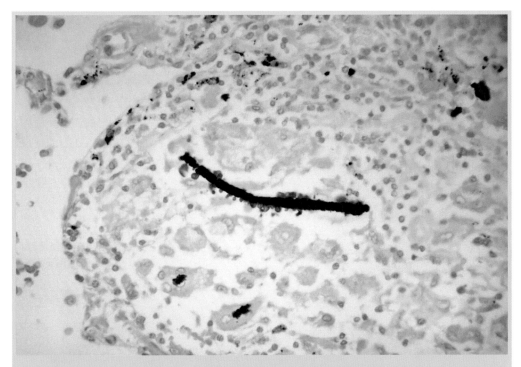

**Figure 6.1** Histopathology of lung showing a ferruginous body stained blue. A fiber of asbestos is coated by an iron-protein complex and surrounded by macrophages. (*CDC/Edwin P. Ewing, Jr.*)

## SPOTLIGHT ON CANCER SCIENTISTS
### ERNEST KENNAWAY (1881–1958)

Ernest Kennaway was born in Exeter, England, in 1881. He received his education at universities in London, Middlesex, and Oxford, earning degrees in five areas of study. He studied biochemistry and the reliability of methods for diagnosing syphilis, among other problems. He did not turn his attention to cancer research until a bit later in his life; he was 41 when he published his first paper on experimental carcinogenesis. After that he focused his energies on the problem of cancer.

By the beginning of the twentieth century, coal tar, soot, and related oils had long been suspected of playing a role in the development of certain cancers. After Katsusaburo Yamagiwa and Koichi Ichikawa successfully induced cancer in rabbits by the repeated application of coal tar, scientists wanted to determine what exactly was in coal tar that caused cancer. Initial research on this question was done by Bruno Bloch and W. Dreifuss, two Swiss scientists who showed in 1921 that they could boil coal tar and concentrate the cancer-causing "factor." Ernest Kennaway, already a well-respected pathologist, decided to study this factor to find out what it was. In 1930 after painstaking chemical purification, Kennaway succeeded in isolating and identifying the molecule: dibenzanthracene. He tested the isolated, purified molecule and found that it

## ASBESTOS

One of the best understood occupational carcinogens is asbestos. A naturally occurring material, asbestos enjoyed widespread use because of its fire resistance, ability to retain heat, and great durability. In the

was carcinogenic. He then chemically synthesized the molecule and showed that it, too, caused cancer. Kennaway had succeeded in demonstrating that cancers could be caused by a specific molecule found in the environment.

In addition to his groundbreaking identification of a specific carcinogenic molecule, Kennaway did a lot of work aimed at identifying the relationship between chemical structures and their carcinogenicity. He also undertook several epidemiological studies that asked questions about cancer incidence in different races; cancer incidences in different occupations; the anatomical distribution of various occupational cancers; the role of socioeconomic status and the incidences of cancers of the scrotum and penis; and the incidences of lung and larynx cancers and their relationships to air pollution and smoking.

Kennaway continued to work at his research for the rest of his life. He was a man of great integrity and perseverance. Upon his retirement in 1946, Kennaway was offered a small set of rooms in the attic of St. Bartholomew's Hospital. There he continued his research, helped by his wife, Nina, whose assistance became even more necessary toward the end of his life, when Kennaway suffered from Parkinson's disease. Kennaway continued to publish his findings until the end of his life in 1958. Together with his wife, Ernest Kennaway established a large part of the foundation of the study of carcinogenesis.

United States, asbestos was used extensively during and after World War II in both shipbuilding and construction. Despite its usefulness as an insulator and building material, asbestos has a terrible side effect. Inhalation of its fibers causes lung cancer as well as **mesothelioma**, a rare cancer of the **pleural covering** of the lungs and **peritoneum**, the lining of the abdominal cavity. Even a transient exposure to a small amount of asbestos can be deadly. The lifetime risk of cancer is quite high in exposed individuals because the fibers remain in the lungs after inhalation; the body cannot effectively clear them out. Although the precise details of the mechanism whereby asbestos causes cancer is not entirely understood, it probably involves chronic inflammation of lung tissue and subsequent DNA damage.

Concerns about worker exposure to asbestos were first articulated in 1930. Studies done between 1930 and 1959 showed that factory workers who were exposed to asbestos developed an inflammatory disease called **asbestosis**. In 1938 the U.S. Public Health Service established the first occupational guidelines for asbestos use. By 1955 it was evident that the range of health problems associated with asbestos was even more dire than asbestosis: Lung cancer was also caused by asbestos exposure. In 1960, a physician in South Africa showed that mesothelioma could be caused by even a low-dose exposure to airborne asbestos. Finally in 1972 the U.S. Occupational Health and Safety Administration (OSHA) began to regulate workplace exposure to asbestos. Unfortunately since the time between the actual exposure to asbestos and death from malignant mesothelioma can be up to 40 years, the deadly outcomes of earlier exposures are still unfolding. They can, however, be expected to level off now that asbestos is no longer being used in the United States and other developed nations.

The problem of asbestos in developing nations is more severe, since asbestos use continues without regulation. In developing countries the tragic health consequences will soon become apparent and will continue to rise for many years to come. Let's consider some numbers to put this situation in perspective. Epidemiologists estimate that by 2020, cancer caused by exposure to asbestos will kill more than one million people in Europe, North America, and other developed nations. The International Labor Office predicts that another one million people in developing nations will die from asbestos-caused malignancies by 2020. At that time, if not sooner, the number of deaths attributed to asbestos will begin to decline in developed countries, while it will continue to rise in developing areas of the world.

The sad part of the asbestos story is that much of the suffering and death could have been avoided entirely. People recognized the dangers of asbestos long before safety measures were put into place. In fact it is clear from company documents that the two main manufacturers of asbestos purposely concealed information regarding the health threats faced by their workers[3]. Furthermore during World War II the U.S. Navy hid the health dangers experienced by 4.5 million shipyard workers who were exposed to asbestos. In the 1960s, a study showed high rates of lung cancer in asbestos insulation workers. This triggered a series of articles in the early 1970s in the *New Yorker* magazine, which focused public attention on the problem. Eventually asbestos use in the United States stopped and the revelation of the "cover-up" inspired a large number of endangered workers to file lawsuits.

Although smoking is the principal cause of lung cancer, smoking and asbestos together have multiplicative effects. Asbestos exposure alone increases the chance of lung cancer five-fold; smoking increases the risk ten-fold. Smoking and asbestos exposure together increase the risk fifty-fold.

## ENVIRONMENTAL CARCINOGENS AND POLLUTION

Given the dramatic and serious effects that occupational exposure to carcinogens can have on health, it is no wonder that many people worry that they are being exposed to dangerous by-products of industry. After all, we have seen that concentrated exposure to certain chemicals can produce cancer in workers. Should we also be concerned that exposure to lower amounts of these same chemicals alone or in combination with others could be harmful as well?

The answer to this question is partly yes. The answer is yes because any increased incidence of cancer in a population, no matter how small, can have dreadful consequences for individuals. Even if the risk of an event was one in 1,000, no one wants to be the unfortunate "one." The answer is "partly yes" because, unlike tobacco and diet, which contribute to more than 65 percent of all cancer deaths in the United States, approximately 2 percent of all cancer deaths are caused by the air, water, and soil pollution. This number is an educated estimate. It is difficult to determine a firm number because the cancers that are caused by pollution, primarily of the bladder or lung, are probably the result of exposure to more than one carcinogen, each at low levels. It is also possible that there are more pollutants that are human carcinogens, but we are not able to detect them because of the comparatively large background cancer levels found in the population. In other words cancer is sufficiently common in the population that it can be hard to determine whether a particular pollutant increases the cancer level further. In any case, as far as we know right now, the vast majority of cancers are caused by external factors, such as smoking, excessive sun exposure, and diet. Yet even 2 percent of cancer deaths by pollution is too high. This problem needs to be addressed.

## PESTICIDES

Of all the possible chemicals to which people may be exposed, the category that provokes perhaps the greatest public concern is pesticides. Although the number of cancer deaths that can be attributed to pesticides is very low—certainly less than 1 percent—susceptibility appears to be greater in children than adults. The first suggestions that pesticide exposure may increase the risk of cancer in children were made in the late 1970s. Since that time many studies have explored this question. The results are somewhat difficult to interpret, but they are quite provocative. One study showed that, compared to children without leukemia, children with leukemia were three times more likely to have had professional exterminators come to their homes to eliminate pests. The same study also showed that a woman's exposure to any pesticide in her home made it twice as likely that her child would develop leukemia, compared to a woman who had not been exposed to pesticide. In a different study, scientists showed that children who lived in a home where pest strips, household pesticides, or garden pesticides were used were more likely to develop cancer than children with no pesticide exposure. An association was found between pesticide use and the development of brain tumors in children.

Also of concern is an association between a parent's occupational exposure to pesticides and childhood cancer. In one study, scientists showed that the risk for Hodgkin's lymphoma was 2.5 times greater in the children of farm workers who applied pesticides. If parents did not wear gloves while applying the pesticides, their children's risk was higher; for those children whose parents did wear gloves, the risk was lower.

It appears likely that pesticide exposure does increase the risk of certain childhood cancers. However, it is important to keep in mind that, even in an exposed population, the development of cancer in response to pesticides is very rare. In some ways this rarity actually seems surprising. In 1999 more than one billion pounds (454 million kg) of pesticide were used in the United States alone. More than 5.6 billion pounds (2.5 billion kg) were applied worldwide. Pesticides are detectable in our homes and even in our bodies, yet only two populations seem to be at most risk: The children and workers who receive massive occupational exposures seem to exhibit increased risk for cancer. Why is this so?

## WHY ARE PEOPLE AFFECTED DIFFERENTLY BY CARCINOGENS?

Not everyone exposed to even a potent carcinogen like tobacco or intense X rays will develop cancer. In a large population that breathes in polluted air, only a small fraction will develop a fatal cancer as a direct result of that exposure. What accounts for this variability?

First, many, if not all, carcinogens act by mutating or changing DNA. In 1938 the chemical carcinogen 3-methylcholanthrene (a product created by roasting meat at high temperatures) was shown to be mutagenic. Since then scientists have demonstrated that many carcinogens are indeed mutagenic. For a mutagen to cause cancer, however, specific parts of DNA need to be altered. Other DNA changes won't produce cancer. Sometimes exposure to carcinogens does not effectively produce damage in the appropriate regions of DNA, so cancer does not result, although other ill effects can still occur.

Another reason why carcinogen exposure does not always cause cancer has to do with what the body does to ingested or inhaled materials. Typically whatever enters our bodies and gets into the bloodstream eventually travels to the liver. There, molecules are broken down and, in many cases, detoxified, meaning chemically altered so that they are no longer harmful to the body. Ironically, in some cases, the liver can turn a chemical that was not directly carcinogenic into one that is. The biochemical pathways for liver metabolism are not the same in all species. This is why animal testing of carcinogens can give different results, depending upon the types of organisms used. For example, in the early 1960s, experiments showed that the chemical 2-acetylaminofluorene (2AAF) was carcinogenic in mice but *not* in guinea pigs. The reason for this difference is simple: Guinea pigs do not have the enzyme needed to break down 2AAF. It is actually the breakdown product, not the 2AAF itself, that is the carcinogen. Consequently, when exposed to 2AAF, mice produce a carcinogenic product, but guinea pigs do not. Just as species can have enzyme differences like this that account for their differences in developing particular cancers, there might also be differences in the biochemistry of individual people that explain some of the variability in human cancers. These individual differences in biochemistry can be due to inherited variability and/or physiological differences in the body produced by lifestyle choices.

## SUMMARY

Exposure to carcinogens in the workplace is a problem for many people. It is important to be aware of the potential and actual carcinogens that might be present and to minimize risk by using safety equipment and appropriate behaviors to limit exposure. All people—but some more than others—are exposed to air, water, and soil pollution. Approximately 2 percent of cancer deaths in the United States can be attributed to pollution. Pesticides seem to be a significant carcinogen for children but not for adults. All people are exposed to environmental carcinogens of one type or another. Yet, for several reasons, most people do not develop cancers as a result.

# 7

## CAN CANCER BE INHERITED?

**KEY POINTS**

♦ Certain cancers seem to run in families.

♦ Hereditary cancers are those where a faulty gene has been inherited or a normal gene is missing. A person who inherits a faulty gene will not necessarily develop cancer, but the probability is high.

♦ There are genes that influence one's susceptibility to cancer.

♦ Genes alone do not determine whether cancers form. Many other factors are involved.

♦ The vast majority of cancers are not caused by single inherited genes.

## THE MYSTERIOUS CASE OF NAPOLEON

Who or what killed Napoleon Bonaparte, the emperor of France who lived from 1769 to 1821? Many people have speculated that he was murdered by poison during his forced exile on the island of St. Helena. Napoleon himself complained that the foul climate of the island and hired English assassins were making him ill. Even so, Napoleon must have had other ideas about what was causing his terrible stomach pain, because he ordered that an autopsy be performed after his death. The final examination of Napoleon's remains was done on his own billiard table by two physicians—one his Corsican doctor, Antommarchi, and the other a Scottish naval surgeon named Archibald Arnott. Although British medical personnel were present, Napoleon's instructions were clear—no English hands should touch him. The results of the autopsy were unequivocal: Napoleon's stomach was riddled with cancerous tumors.

What made Napoleon want to have his cause of death determined accurately? Even though Napoleon had cast suspicions on the English, he also worried about another possible explanation for his illness. Napoleon's father had died of stomach cancer and the similarity of the symptoms made Napoleon worry that he, too, was dying of the disease. The reason he ordered the autopsy was to see whether stomach cancer was indeed his problem so that his own son could know and perhaps avoid this painful disease. Evidently stomach cancer did not confine itself to Napoleon and his father. One of his sisters definitely died from the disease, and it is likely that a grandfather, one brother, and two other sisters had it, too. As Napoleon had feared, people in his family had an inherited predisposition to cancer, meaning that they had a greater likelihood of developing the disease than people who came from families where the disease was not present in relatives.

## FAMILIAL CANCERS

People, both before and since Napoleon, have observed that some cancers seem to run in families. In fact there are relatively few situations

## SPOTLIGHT ON CANCER SCIENTISTS
### HENRY LYNCH (1928-  )

Born in 1928 in Lawrence, Massachusetts, Henry Lynch has taken a somewhat unconventional path toward becoming a world-class cancer researcher. Lynch quit high school in order to join the Navy and fight in World War II, but because he was only 16 years old, Lynch "borrowed" his cousin's identification and lied about his age to the recruiter. The Navy found out about Lynch's deception but let him stay in the Navy under his own name. Lynch served in both the Atlantic and Pacific theaters of the war, but most of his time was spent as a gunner on a ship in the Pacific Ocean. Lynch was part of the force that liberated the Philippines.

After the war Lynch left the Navy and worked as a professional boxer for a while. Eventually he took an exam to complete his high school requirements and enrolled at the

**Figure 7.1** Henry Lynch. (*Creighton University Media Services*)

where an inherited defective gene causes cancer. For example, 5 to 10 percent of some common cancers, such as breast, colon, ovary, prostate, melanoma, and thyroid cancer, may involve inherited mutations. Such

University of Oklahoma. He continued his education and he earned his medical degree from the University of Texas–Galveston. He became an expert in both human genetics and cancer.

In 1967 Lynch joined the faculty of Creighton University Medical School in Nebraska. In the 1960s and early 1970s he demonstrated clearly that inheritance plays a role in some cancers. Specifically Lynch found that some families exhibit an inheritance pattern for breast and ovarian cancers. This disorder is now known as hereditary breast/ovarian cancer (HBOC) syndrome.

At the time of Lynch's discovery, the research community was not especially interested in, or convinced about, the importance of genetics in cancer. Instead scientists were much more focused on cancer-causing viruses. Nonetheless Lynch continued his laboratory and clinical work. He kept documenting the causes of all breast tumors and their specific physical locations in all families that exhibited breast cancer. In doing so, he created the largest resource of its kind in the world. Lynch's records were critical for the work that was ultimately done to identify the specific genes that are responsible for HBOC.

In addition to HBOC, Lynch has also studied a variety of other hereditary cancers, including certain malignancies of the colon, rectum, pancreas, and skin. And the scientific community has finally caught up to Lynch. In recent years, he has received a number of well-deserved awards and accolades.

inherited cancers are therefore rare; 90 to 95 percent of the cancers are nonfamilial. However, two important understandings emerge from the revelation that some cancers are inherited. First, this finding shows that genes are important for tumor formation. Second, these familial cancers offer a way to use the tools in genetics and molecular biology to determine *which* genes are important for cancer development.

Normal DNA function is necessary for avoiding cancer. The carcinogenic agents that have been discussed in previous chapters all have one critical thing in common—every one of them damages DNA in some way that impairs cell function. It is no real surprise, then, to see that a person who inherits faulty versions of genes or might even be missing key genes could be vulnerable to developing cancer if these genes were important for normal cell proliferation and behavior.

As discussed earlier cancers generally do not have a single cause. The sum total of a person's genes, the individual's exposure to carcinogens, lifestyle choices, and chance play a role in whether an invasive tumor will form. For some people inherited cancer susceptibility genes are part of the picture. But even for these individuals, other factors, including other genes, come into play to determine whether cancer will form. The next section will consider the specific case of a gene that can cause a familial cancer of the retina (the part of the eye that detects light and color) called **retinoblastoma**.

## Retinoblastoma

At first, Emma's parents thought she had a "lazy" eye. Her two eyes would not focus together. An examination of four-month-old Emma by a pediatric ophthalmologist revealed shocking news: She had six tumors in each eye. The doctor explained to Emma's parents that such tumors are always malignant and that action needed to be taken quickly. Emma underwent more than 30 surgeries and four rounds of chemotherapy, a type of medical treatment used to eliminate cancer cells. After these treatments Emma's right eye was doing very well.

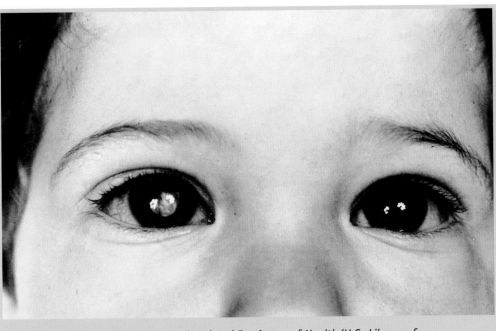

**Figure 7.2** Retinoblastoma. *(National Institutes of Health/U.S. Library of Medicine)*

Unfortunately things did not work out so well for her left eye. A new set of tumors eventually developed and Emma had to have her left eye removed. This surgery was done a few months before she turned five years old. The surgery was a physical challenge for Emma and an emotional one for her and her family. Now seven years old, Emma is doing well. She is the proud owner of a new prosthetic eye. She is happy, enjoys life, and is only disappointed that her friends won't believe that she has a fake eye.

The type of cancer Emma had, retinoblastoma, is a relatively rare tumor of the retina. This disease affects approximately one child in

20,000. Generally, retinoblastoma appears in children younger than five years, usually before the age of two years. This cancer accounts for 3 percent of all childhood cancers that occur before the age of 15. If left untreated, retinoblastoma is usually fatal. Worldwide, 87 percent of children with this disease die from it. In developed nations, the availability of early detection and treatment means that 90 percent of children who develop retinoblastoma can be cured. Unfortunately many of these surviving children will experience moderate to severe loss of vision.

Approximately 30 to 40 percent of all retinoblastoma cases are inherited. In other words, there is a genetic defect within families that is passed on to offspring in each generation. The remaining cases (60 to 70 percent) occur in children for whom there is no family history of the disease. The inherited version of retinoblastoma is typically much more serious—tumors usually form in both eyes, whereas the nonhereditary form usually causes a single tumor to develop in one eye. Tumors also appear at a younger age in children with hereditary retinoblastoma than they do in children with the nonhereditary form of the disease.

What accounts for the differences in severity between the hereditary and nonhereditary forms of retinoblastoma? This question was studied in the early 1970s by the American scientist and physician Alfred Knudsen who noticed that more bilateral cases of retinoblastoma—where both eyes have tumors—occurred in younger children than did unilateral cases, where only one eye was affected. Knudsen also saw that hereditary retinoblastoma tends to be bilateral. Using this information, Knudsen proposed his "two-hit" hypothesis. Since we all inherit two copies of the gene for any characteristic—one from the mother and one from the father—it would take two hits, or mutations, to disable both copies of a given gene. According to Knudsen, children with hereditary retinoblastoma inherited one faulty gene from one parent and a good copy from the other. As a consequence, in these children, only one "hit," or mutation, is necessary for both genes to be disabled completely, resulting in retinoblastoma. In contrast, children with nonhereditary retinoblastoma inherited two good copies of the gene. In order to develop retinoblastoma, two mutations are needed to render both copies of the gene nonfunctional. Knudsen's hypothesis was very exciting because it suggested that tumors could form if both copies of a single gene were inactivated.

Since Knudsen's groundbreaking work, other scientists have developed the molecular biological methods to examine DNA directly. Using these tools, we have learned a great deal about the retinoblastoma gene. First, **cytogenetic** analysis—the examination of the structure of chromosomes in cells—revealed that the retinoblastoma gene (*Rb*) is located in a specific region of chromosome 13. Moreover, the specific retinoblastoma gene has been isolated. In *all* patients with hereditary retinoblastoma, the *Rb* gene is either mutated or deleted (missing). This is also true for the majority of people with nonhereditary retinoblastoma. Finally, the biochemical function of the *Rb* gene has been elucidated: It is a **tumor suppressor** gene that functions to regulate cell division directly. When the *Rb* gene is missing or deactivated, cell division is not under normal control and tumors can result. Evidently, normal *Rb* genes function as tumor suppressors in the retina. Abnormal *Rb* genes fail to suppress tumor formation. Mutations of the *Rb* gene are implicated in other types of cancers as well. Still, the *Rb* gene is particularly critical for the development of retinoblastoma. Inheriting a defective *Rb* gene increases the risk of developing retinoblastoma from one in 100,000 to 90,000 in 100,000. Even in this type of case, it can be seen that the disease is still not 100 percent certain to develop. As mentioned earlier, cancer causation is a multifaceted phenomenon that is not generally attributable to a single cause, which means that completely accurate predictions regarding the fate of any one individual cannot be made.

## Breast Cancer

In 1866, French physician Paul Broca wondered whether there was a hereditary component to the breast cancer that was prevalent in his wife's family. He mapped a **pedigree** of her relatives that showed the undeniable cluster of cases within the family. In all, 10 out of 24 women, including Broca's wife, had breast cancer. As is the case for retinoblastoma, individuals can inherit mutant genes that dramatically increase their risk of developing cancer. In contrast to retinoblastoma, however, the breast cancer story is less well understood and appears to be more complex.

Except for non-melanoma skin cancer, breast cancer is the most frequently diagnosed cancer in women in the United States; approximately 12 percent of American women will develop this disease. Breast cancer is also one of the deadliest cancers. Only lung cancer has a higher fatality rate. Epidemiologists estimate that in 2005 there will be 212,930 new cases and 40,870 deaths from breast cancer. Many external factors increase the risk for developing breast cancer, including exposure to ionizing radiation, a high-fat diet, early age of puberty and late age of menopause, and not having children. Breast cancer is more prevalent in women who live in developed, affluent societies than it is in women who live in developing areas of the world.

Along with these potential external causes of breast cancer, there are internal genetic features to consider as well. With respect to the inheritance of breast cancer, there are three categories: sporadic, familial,

**Figure 7.3** Paul Broca. (*National Institutes of Health/U.S. Library of Medicine*)

and hereditary. In at least 90 percent of breast cancers, there is no known inherited gene that causes the cancer. Women in this category have no strong family history of breast cancer. This type of breast cancer is called

## SPOTLIGHT ON CANCER SCIENTISTS
### MARY-CLAIRE KING (1946– )

Born in Illinois in 1946, Mary-Claire King was a math major at Carleton College in Minnesota and studied biology at the University of California–Berkeley, during the politically turbulent 1960s. When Governor Ronald Reagan sent the National Guard to clear protesting students out of the college buildings they were occupying, King dropped out of her graduate program and took a job working for consumer advocate and political candidate Ralph Nader, where she studied the effects of pesticides on farm workers. Encouraged to continue her studies by Allan Wilson, her professor at Berkeley, King decided to return to graduate school. Together, King and Wilson examined the genes of humans and chimpanzees and showed that 99 percent of the genes were common to both species. Next, King turned her attention to the idea of looking for single genes that are important in human disease. When she first started this work, many other scientists thought she was foolish. Geneticists just did not think it was possible that a complex disease could be associated with a specific gene. In 1990, after 16 years of work, King announced that she had discovered *BRCA-1*, the gene responsible for hereditary breast cancer, and that she had mapped it to a particular location on chromosome 17. Since then, other scientists have linked Alzheimer's disease and prostate cancer to single mutations in specific susceptibility genes.

Mary-Claire King has also used her talents as a scientist to make other contributions. She was part of a group that did forensics work on mass graves in the former Yugoslavia, attempting to identify the remains of hundreds of people who were probably victims of genocide. She also continues work she began in 1984 with the *Abuelas de Plaza de Mayo*, a group of grandmothers from Argentina who are tracking the whereabouts of children whose parents disappeared during Argentina's military dictatorship in the 1970s and early 1980s. The par-

**Figure 7.4** Mary-Claire King. (*Courtesy of Mary-Claire King, PhD*)

ents of these children were killed and the children themselves were left in orphanages or illegally adopted by military families. King uses DNA analysis to identify the children (who are now in their twenties and thirties) and reunite them with their grandparents.

In addition King has been studying the genetic basis for deafness. She and her colleagues have made a good start by isolating one of the genes involved. She has also undertaken an extensive project with collaborators in both Palestine and Israel to try to find the genes that are responsible for deafness. This example of peaceful cooperation between Palestinians and Israelis is thanks, in some part, to the efforts and scientific vision of Mary-Claire King.

**sporadic**. In **familial** breast cancer, hereditary factors—although not a specific, identifiable gene—may interact with environmental factors to cause breast cancer. Some 15 to 20 percent of breast cancers fall into this category. Women in this group have no strong family history of breast cancer, but they may have had a case here or there in the family. For these women, any inherited component increases the predisposition for breast cancer, but external agents are also required. Finally, **hereditary** breast cancer accounts for 5 to 10 percent of all breast cancer cases. Women in this group have a very strong family history, meaning that they have multiple family members from either their mother's or father's side of the family, from multiple generations, who developed breast cancer. It is likely that Paul Broca's wife came from a family that had hereditary breast cancer.

Unlike the situation for sporadic or familial breast cancer, scientists have been able to identify specific inherited genes that increase dramatically the likelihood of developing breast cancer. American scientist Mary-Claire King's research group identified the first, *BRCA-1*, and showed that this gene is located on chromosome 17. In 1994 another team of scientists isolated the *BRCA-1* gene and determined its exact structure. A second gene associated with hereditary breast cancer, *BRCA-2*, was also identified and described. Together, *BRCA-1* and *BRCA-2* account for 90 percent of all hereditary breast cancers (and up to 5 to 10 percent of all breast cancers in the general population). Individuals who have mutant *BRCA* genes face likelihoods as high as 84 percent that they will develop breast cancer by the age of 70.

What are the functions of the *BRCA-1* and *BRCA-2* genes, and why does damaging them dramatically increase the risk of breast cancer?

So far, scientists have figured out two important jobs that the *BRCA-1* gene do in cells. First, similar to what we discussed with respect to the *Rb* (retinoblastoma) gene, *BRCA-1* regulates normal cell division. A cell with a mutant *BRCA-1* gene has the potential to proliferate in an uncontrolled manner. *BRCA-1* is also important for DNA repair. When DNA is damaged, cells have repair mechanisms that can sometimes fix the mutation. A mutant *BRCA-1* gene does not repair DNA effectively and, as a consequence, DNA damage and errors can result in mutations that lead to cancer. *BRCA-2* is also necessary for DNA repair. As with *BRCA-1*, a mutant version of the *BRCA-2* gene will enable cells to accumulate DNA damage and mutations.

## INHERITANCE, GENES, AND CANCER

Despite the vivid examples of inherited cancers such as hereditary retinoblastoma and breast cancer, it is important to remember that the vast majority of cancers, probably 99 percent, are not due to single inherited genes. Instead, many factors interact to determine the overall risk that people face in regard to developing tumors. Most cancers result from a lifetime of accumulated damage to the DNA.

In addition to the specific carcinogens to which people are exposed either accidentally or knowingly, there are genes that modify cancer risk indirectly. For example, how well do "detoxification" genes work? What about DNA repair genes? There are many DNA repair genes in addition to *BRCA-1* and *BRCA-2*. The risk of getting cancer is an interactive combination of genetic inheritance, diet, lifestyle choices, exposure to chemicals and radiation, and chance.

## SUMMARY

Exposure to carcinogens can damage DNA in such a way that genes are altered and cancer develops. In rare cases, people inherit mutant genes that dramatically increase the likelihood that cancer will develop, such as certain retinoblastomas and breast cancers. In other cases people inherit genes that may influence their relative susceptibility to cancer. In no case do genes or the environment act alone. The risk of getting cancer is determined by a combination of genes, environment, personal choice, and chance.

# 8

# CAN CANCER BE PREVENTED?

**KEY POINTS**

- Many cancers are preventable.

- A greater number of lives could be saved with cancer prevention than with treatment.

- Early detection of cancer is important because it increases the likelihood that treatment will be successful.

- There are specific actions you can take to reduce your cancer risk.

## ANOTHER LESSON FROM CHICKENS

In Linxian County, China, the incidence of esophageal cancer is one of the highest in the world. The lifetime risk for developing tumors in the esophagus is almost 10 percent for people in this region in China. In other parts of the world, esophageal cancer is rarer. What factors are responsible for the prevalence of this disease in Linxian County?

Epidemiologists wondered whether the unusual diet consumed by Linxian peasants might be partly responsible. A major component of the local diet consists of vegetables that are boiled and then stored in jars for months. During the time in storage, a layer of mold grows over the top of the vegetable mash. When the jars are opened, this fungal layer is mixed with the mushy vegetables and the entire mix is eaten. Although epidemiologists cannot demonstrate a definite link between eating moldy vegetables and developing esophageal cancer, an association is biologically plausible for several reasons: First, the molds are known to contain carcinogenic nitrosamines. Second, other studies done in Hong Kong have shown a link between the consumption of pickled vegetables and the development of esophageal cancers. Third, a clear indication that the moldy vegetable mash is carcinogenic comes from an animal "experiment."

The Linxian peasants share their moldy vegetable mash with their chickens, to the detriment of the birds, which develop cancer of the gullet, a structure similar to the human esophagus. Although moldy vegetables could well be the cause, with the information considered so far, one could blame some other factor common to living in Linxian County for the cancers experienced by people and chickens.

A step toward answering the question of why there is so much esophageal cancer in Linxian County came from the relocation of 50,000 peasants from Linxian County to Hubei. When they moved, the Linxians brought their usual diets but left their chickens behind, getting new ones in Hubei. Thousands of these "adopted" chickens were subsequently studied and compared to local chickens that lived with native Hubei families. Results showed that some of the chickens that were living in Hubei but were eating the moldy vegetable mash of their Linxian keepers developed gullet cancer, whereas none of the chickens that ate typical Hubei food did.

The Chinese government, along with the U.S. National Cancer Institute, did a nutritional intervention study. One aspect of this effort was to discourage people from eating the moldy vegetable mash. People were also taught methods of food preservation to minimize fungal growth. In addition to these actions, the Chinese government established an early detection program to screen people for the first stages of esophageal cancer. These efforts appear to be paying off: The mortality rates for esophageal cancer are starting to decrease.

## PREVENTION IS AN IMPORTANT TOOL FOR COMBATING CANCER

In the case described above, a connection was made between the development of esophageal cancer and exposure to an external agent—a moldy vegetable mash. Although we do not know all of the steps in the causal chain, and we do not fully understand the cellular mechanisms by which tumors formed, we can still step in to break the chain and, in many cases, prevent cancer from developing. This scenario is not unique to the case of the Linxian peasants. Whenever the causes or risk factors associated with a disease can be identified, there is a chance to block the causal pathway and prevent the disease. This is true even when it is not entirely understood why these actions work. Although people understandably tend to get most excited when they learn about the successes of new cancer drugs or treatments, the best way to avoid cancer mortality is to prevent cancer in the first place. Epidemiologists estimate that by paying closer attention to cancer prevention instead of focusing primarily on treatment, at least ten times more lives could be saved compared to the number of people who are kept alive by successful cancer treatment. It is also estimated that at least 80 percent of cancers are preventable, at least in principle.

To some people, recognizing that many cancers are avoidable seems like blaming the victim. Actually it might be more correct to see that the knowledge that cancer is preventable is empowering, since it can help people make good choices. In any case, it is clear that prevention of cancer is better than treatment, since it spares people fear, physical pain, and the financial burden of the disease.

## EVIDENCE THAT CANCER IS PREVENTABLE

It is a bold claim to say that the majority of cancers are avoidable. What is the evidence for such an assertion? The data come from several types of epidemiological studies. First, there are cancers that are common in some parts of the world but rare in others. For example cancers of the colon and rectum exhibit more than a ten-fold variation in the rates of incidence worldwide. This might be explained by hypothesizing that there are genetic or environmental factors that contribute to cancer risk. However, the cancer patterns of immigrants follow those of their new environment and not their **gene pool.** Second, there have been dramatic changes in the incidence of certain cancers over time. For example stomach cancer was once the most prevalent cause of cancer mortality in the United States, but it is much less common now. Third, there are examples of social groups within a country who experience much lower cancer incidences than the general population. For instance Mormons have much lower rates of cancer and other diseases than the general population. Fourth, with the exceptions of breast, prostate, colon, and rectal cancers, all other cancers are more prevalent among poor members of society and in poor regions of the world. All of these observations lead to the conclusion that there are environmental factors that influence cancer development. Presumably if we could identify these factors, we should be able to avoid many or even most of them and thereby prevent cancer.

Many causes of cancer have been identified. Is there convincing evidence that avoiding exposure to a carcinogen will actually lower cancer incidence in the population?  Let's look at cigarette smoking and consider this question. As discussed in Chapter 3, cigarette smoking represents one of the biggest "experiments" ever done to test a carcinogen—billions of people have unwittingly participated. As a result, it was learned that cigarette smoke is a potent carcinogen and that the diseases it causes exact significant costs in suffering and life. Studying what happens if smoking is reduced in the population revealed one of the most dramatic success stories for the prevention of a specific cancer.

The story begins in 1950 with the publication in the United States and Great Britain of the first detailed medical reports to link cigarette smoking and cancer. In 1955 the lung cancer incidence rate in British men under the age of 55 was the highest in the world. This enormous incidence in lung cancer was traced to a change in the smoking habits of British men. During and after World War I (1914–1918), smoking increased dramatically in the male population. As a consequence men born around 1900 began to smoke at a younger age and in larger numbers than men born before 1900.

Because of the reported association between smoking and lung cancer, actions were eventually taken to address this serious health problem. British cigarettes were redesigned so that tar levels were reduced. Public health education efforts also produced a marked decrease in the number of people who smoked. As a result of these efforts, the lung cancer rate in British men below the age of 55 dropped by more than 65 percent. These numbers show that prevention can work.

## EARLY DETECTION

Another way to reduce cancer mortality is by early detection. Although prevention is best, the detection of precancerous lesions or early localized cancers enhances the chance of successful treatment. Two types of cancer for which screening and early detection have been particularly successful in reducing mortality are cervical and colorectal (colon and rectum) cancers. For both types of cancer, epidemiologists say that death rates could be reduced by at least 50 percent if screening were more widely available and done more regularly. The reason why early detection is so successful for cervical and colorectal cancers is because precancerous lesions and early malignancies are easily identified and removed. Screening for early stages of skin, breast, and prostate cancer are also successful in identifying cancers at very early stages, when treatment has a better chance of success.

## WHAT CAN YOU DO TO REDUCE YOUR CANCER RISK?

Given that most cancers are, at least in principle, preventable, it makes sense for us to identify ways to avoid exposure to carcinogens. Despite the public's fears about a variety of potential carcinogens, including some that don't actually present a large risk to the general population (for example, uranium), the vast majority of cancer deaths in the United States are due to smoking, an unhealthy diet, and a lack of regular physical activity or exercise, particularly during youth. As one cancer researcher has said, "The best way to avoid cancer is to run from salad bar to salad bar."[4] Epidemiologists have estimated that if we did more to stop risky behaviors, more than 200,000 lives could be saved each year without any new cancer treatments being discovered. That said, here are some specific steps that you can take to reduce your risk of cancer.

1.  *Don't inhale smoke or use tobacco products.* According to British epidemiologist Sir Richard Peto, "If there is no reduction in the sales of tobacco, more people who are alive today are going to die from smoking than the total number who have died in all the wars and revolutions of the 20th century."[5] If you do smoke, quit. Because carcinogens take a long time to transform cells to a cancerous state, quitting will lower your risk compared to that of a smoker and, in many cases, your risk may eventually be as low as that of a person who has never smoked.

2.  *Eat a diet that is rich in fruits, vegetables, and fiber, and low in saturated fat.* You will reduce your risk of several types of cancer, including those of the breast, prostate, colon, and rectum. High-fat diets are associated with an increased risk of these cancers. Eating a diet high in fiber will clear away dead and damaged cells from your digestive system more regularly.

3.  *Avoid excessive exposure to ultraviolet (UV) light.* You don't need to stay indoors—in fact, that would be bad for you, since we do need some UV light in order to produce vitamin D. However, covering up during the most intense periods of sunlight (or staying inside) and being sure not to get a sunburn when you are outside will decrease your risk of skin cancer.

4.  *Be physically active and maintain a healthy weight.* For nonsmokers in the United States, the risk of dying from cancer is directly proportional to the degree you are overweight. Increased body fat increases the risk of breast, colon, and prostate cancers.

5.  *Don't engage in risky sexual behavior such as intercourse without a condom.* Viruses that cause cancer of the cervix and, more rarely, cancer of the penis are transmitted sexually, as are certain viruses that cause a particular type of leukemia seen most frequently in Japan and the Caribbean.

## SPOTLIGHT ON CANCER SCIENTISTS
### C. Everett Koop (1916-  )

Born in Brooklyn, New York, in 1916, C. Everett Koop was six years old when he decided he wanted to be a surgeon. As a boy, Koop practiced tying knots and carefully cutting pictures out of magazines with both hands, figuring that a surgeon would need to be equally dexterous with either hand. At the age of 14, Koop sneaked into the viewing gallery at Columbia University so he could observe surgeries. He spent his summers working at volunteer jobs in local hospitals. In 1933, Koop was accepted to Dartmouth College on a football scholarship. He stopped playing football because of an eye injury. Koop attended medical school at Cornell University and then went to Philadelphia for additional training. He became a surgeon at Children's Hospital in Philadelphia. Koop became an internationally known and respected pediatric surgeon.

In 1981 President Ronald Reagan appointed Koop to be surgeon general of the United States. In this role Koop reinvigorated the morale and motivation of the U.S. Public Heath Service (USPHS). Koop spent the most time on his antismoking campaign. In his first report as surgeon general, Koop connected smoking to cancers of the lung, oral cavity, larynx, esophagus, bladder, pancreas, and kidney. He also provided evidence that the nicotine in tobacco is an addictive substance.

These findings were disputed by the tobacco industry, but Koop responded by criticizing them for spending $4,000 on advertising for every $1 that the U.S. Public Health Service spent on antismoking messages. In

1982 Koop testified before Congress that the surgeon general's warning on cigarettes, which simply stated that smoking is hazardous to one's health, should be changed to mention specific health risks, such as cancer. In 1984 Koop launched the Campaign for a Smoke-Free America by 2000. He urged smokers to quit for their health and encouraged nonsmokers to insist that they should be protected from secondhand smoke. In 1986 Koop got the surgeon general's warning placed on smokeless tobacco and issued a report that showed that secondhand smoke was a health

**Figure 8.1** Former Surgeon General C. Everett Koop shown addressing Centers for Disease Control employees during a 1980s presentation. *(CDC/VEC)*

risk to nonsmokers, especially children. As a result of this work, smoking is now banned in federal buildings, public transportation, and workplaces and restaurants in a growing number of states.

Coop's antismoking campaign was very successful. In 1981, at the start of Koop's term, 33 percent of Americans smoked. Smoking killed 400,000 Americans in 1981, more than the combined number of deaths due to alcohol, drug abuse, and car accidents. By 1989, thanks to the work of Koop and others, only 26 percent of Americans smoked.

6. *Avoid excessive alcohol consumption.* The potential carcinogenic effects of alcohol are more frequently seen if a person both drinks and smokes to excess.

7. *Don't expose yourself to known carcinogens at work or in the environment, including your home.* For example, if you handle carcinogenic materials at work, use protective equipment. At home, be aware of the chemicals and solvents you use and take appropriate precautions for safe use. Also make sure that your home does not have dangerous levels of radon.

These steps should be seen as empowering. You have a lot of control over your well-being. Even so, some cancers are inevitable. The disease is complex and is the result of interactions between many factors, both internal and external. Chance also plays a role. So, even though people can do a lot to reduce their risks, it is important to realize that if a cancer does develop, no one is to blame.

## SUMMARY

The number of deaths due to cancer can be decreased by preventing the disease or detecting problems at a precancerous or very early stage so that treatment has a greater likelihood of success. Although we can't eliminate all cancers, we can prevent most with some very straightforward actions.

# 9

# QUESTIONS AND CHALLENGES
# FOR THE FUTURE

**KEY POINTS**

- We need to rethink the problem of cancer causation and cure.

- Research is under way to develop and test vaccines directed against carcinogenic pathogens.

- Chemoprevention uses natural or synthetic materials to prevent or stop tumor development.

- It may eventually be possible to screen people for cancer susceptibility genes and to evaluate the genes of tumor cells to help with diagnosis and treatment.

- Being poor increases a person's risk of cancer.

# RETHINKING CANCER

Understanding of the causes of cancer and possible ways to prevent this disease has grown tremendously, particularly since the middle of the twentieth century, thanks to the successes of both epidemiological and laboratory studies. One thing we have learned is that the search for a single cause for cancer is probably futile. According to cancer researcher Dr. Mel Greaves, "[the] erroneous perceptions of the existence of *a* cause and the possibility of *a* cure have fuelled unrealistic expectations. . . . Ionizing radiation is the only known cause of breast cancer. . . . But it clearly isn't *the* cause of these cancers or even involved in anything but a small minority of them."[6] It is critical to recognize that cancer causation is multifaceted—chance and many genetic and environmental factors  interact over time to influence whether a tumor forms. Moreover, it is probably necessary to reconceptualize the view of a cancer cure. Although there have been significant breakthroughs in the treatment of some cancers—for example, childhood leukemia, Hodgkin's disease, and testicular cancer—many other cancers continue to be fatal for many people. The total number of cancer deaths in men in the United States declined for the first time in the late 1990s after many decades of data collection, which is welcome, although this decline is probably more due to early detection than to advances in cancer treatment. Clearly the prevention of cancer is the best strategy for saving lives. In the future we may control cancer more by prevention than by treatment, just as we presently try to manage certain infectious diseases and cardiovascular conditions.

In those situations where cancers do occur—and some always will, no matter how much the risk is reduced—treatments will certainly be done to eliminate tumors and cancer cells. However, it may not always be possible to remove or destroy *every* cancer cell and it may not be necessary to do so. In some cases it may be appropriate to think of cancer as a chronic, manageable condition, much as doctors now view diabetes or cardiovascular disease. In the not-too-distant past, these diseases were quickly fatal. Although it is critical for scientists to continue to work on identifying cancer causes, preventions, and treatments, rethinking the entire problem is also essential for progress.

## VACCINES FOR CANCER-CAUSING INFECTIOUS AGENTS

As we have already seen, 15 to 20 percent of cancers worldwide are caused by infections by viruses, bacteria, or parasites. A very promising future possibility is that vaccines will be developed to protect people from cancer-causing pathogens. For the hepatitis B virus (HBV), a major cause of liver cancer throughout the world, the future is now: A vaccine has been developed, tested, and is widely available. The vaccine Gardasil, has been recently approved of for use by the FDA for the human papillomavirus (HPV), which causes cervical cancer; vaccines are also being developed for hepatitis C virus (HCV), which causes liver cancer, and the Epstein-Barr virus, which causes nasopharyngeal cancer and some lymphomas. Laboratory studies and clinical trials are under way for these vaccines, but a lot more work needs to be done to develop safe and effective vaccines that can be administered efficiently to large populations.

Besides vaccines, another effective way to prevent infection is to stop the transmission or spread of the virus, bacteria, or parasite that causes cancer. Fortunately the modes of transmission are well understood for many carcinogenic organisms. For example both HBV and HCV are found in blood. Consequently screening blood supplies for these viruses prevents transmission through blood transfusions. Also human thymus-derived-cell leukemia/lymphoma virus-1 (HTLV-1), which causes leukemia in adults in Japan and the Caribbean, is transmitted through human body fluids. Avoiding risky sexual behaviors, such as sexual intercourse without using a condom, will reduce the spread of this pathogen. Some of the organisms, such as *Helicobacter pylori*, schistosomes, and flukes, are spread in poor areas because of the lack of clean water.

Although prevention is better, successful treatment of a cancer-causing pathogen is a worthwhile goal. Studies have shown that treatment with antibiotics produces a **remission** and may even cure gastric lymphoma caused by *H. pylori* infections. **Antibiotics** have induced the remission of stomach cancers if the tumors were not too advanced. Future research in this area will focus on the development of drugs to combat carcinogenic pathogens.

## CHEMOPREVENTION

In the 1950s some scientists began research in **chemoprevention**, a way to prevent cancer by using natural or manufactured materials to prevent or halt carcinogenesis. Chemoprevention is probably best seen as one component of an overall prevention program in which an individual will have a cancer risk evaluation and receive expert recommendations about lifestyle changes. Chemopreventative agents include **phytochemicals**, which are components derived from plant foods, hormones, and drugs. This area of research has blossomed over the years. Many materials have been and are still being tested in laboratory experiments and, in some cases, epidemiological studies.

Let's consider the phytochemical dithiolthione as an example of this approach to cancer prevention. Found in cruciferous vegetables such as broccoli, cabbage, and cauliflower, dithiolthione has been shown experimentally to inhibit the development of tumors of the lung, colon, mammary glands, and bladder in laboratory animals. Scientists have a good hypothesis about how this phytochemical interferes with carcinogenesis: Dithiolthione activates liver enzymes that, in turn, detoxify carcinogens that make it into the bloodstream.

The search for chemopreventative agents has yielded some good results and many promising leads for future research. For instance taking a baby aspirin daily can prevent colon cancer in some adults. Epidemiological and experimental studies have demonstrated that eating raw or cooked garlic decreases the risks of stomach and colorectal cancers. The spices saffron and turmeric, tea, and flaxseed all contain phytochemicals that protect against cancer. Some of these materials are being tested in clinical trials.

A lot of research has shown that a diet rich in fruits, vegetables, and fiber, and low in animal fat reduces the risk of developing several types of cancer. A challenge for scientists is to identify which phytochemicals have chemopreventative ability and a way to deliver them to people in a safe way over long time intervals. This approach is particularly important in those cases where eating a varied, well-balanced diet is not possible because of food availability or costs, or for people in high-risk groups for whom a good diet alone may not be sufficient protection.

## SCREENING FOR CANCER GENES

Exploring the genes that are involved in carcinogenesis is an important step for the development of new tools to screen for cancer genes. If doctors could examine cancer genes directly, they could do a better job of preventing, detecting, and treating this disease. Two categories of genes could be screened to good effect. Even now the DNA of high-risk individuals can be examined to see if they have mutant genes for

## SPOTLIGHT ON CANCER SCIENTISTS
### MICHAEL SPORN (1933-  )

Compared to many other cancer research scientists, Michael Sporn of Dartmouth Medical School is a bit of a maverick. His focus is not so much on a cure for cancer as it is on the prevention of the disease. In fact Sporn thinks that physicians and research scientists need to redirect their attentions toward stopping cancer before it starts rather than devoting resources to treatment of the end stage. He argues that the disease we should be fighting is carcinogenesis—the gradual, multistep process by which cells change to produce malignant cancers. Sporn believes that

**Figure 9.1**  Michael Sporn. *(Courtesy of Michael B. Sporn, M.D.)*

cancer, like cardiovascular disease, often results from the accumulation of many years of unhealthy living. As with heart disease, early intervention and prevention may be successful strategies for saving lives.

Because the development of a full-blown metastatic cancer involves many changes, often over a long time period, Sporn's idea is to create ways to detect and stop the development of the cancer early on. Just as cardiovascular disease and strokes can be prevented by monitoring and controlling blood cholesterol, blood lipids, and blood pressure, we could do the same thing for cancer if we had accurate tests for the biochemical changes that happen in cells during the early stages of carcinogenesis. Sporn coined the term *chemoprevention* to describe the approach of using nutritional supplements, modified diets, or drugs to prevent the development of cancer. In his research, Sporn has shown that **retinoids**, molecules related to vitamin A and **beta-carotene**, are able to inhibit tumor development. He is also examining the actions of several possible chemopreventative agents, including molecules related to vitamin D, drugs that modify cellular responses to the hormone estrogen, and a series of synthetic compounds related to retinoids. Sporn has identified some treatments that have successfully stopped cancer progression in laboratory tests. The National Cancer Institute (NCI) is now sponsoring clinical trials of some chemopreventative substances to see if they can stop cancer from developing in people. It will be exciting to see how these studies turn out, but for now Sporn's biggest challenge still remains: to convince more scientists to devote their energy to stopping carcinogenesis in its tracks and therefore preventing cancer from developing at all.

inherited cancers, such as certain retinoblastomas and breast cancers. The information learned from such tests is helpful for ensuring early detection and the treatment of cancers should they develop. In the future it may be possible to identify more cancer susceptibility genes in all people and, in so doing, determine individual risk and design appropriate prevention strategies.

The second type of genetic screening that might be beneficial would be to look at the genes found in tumors and identify those that indicate the degree of malignancy or how serious and invasive the tumor might be. Looking at the activity of tumor mutant genes might permit doctors to find ways to detect cancer earlier and to figure out which cancers may be the most potentially serious. A genetic profile of a tumor might provide information for the design of effective treatments for individual cancers.

Creating genetic profiles of tumors to help diagnosis and treatment is something that may be done in the future. However, there may already be another strategy—targeting the abnormal proteins that cancer cells make—that is turning out to be successful. One example that uses this approach is the drug Herceptin. Clinical trials have shown that this drug enhances the usual treatments for some breast cancers. Herceptin works by disabling an abnormal protein found on the cell surfaces of approximately 30 percent of malignant, invasive breast cancer cells. Another example is Gleevec, a drug that has successfully treated early (but not late) stages of chronic myelogenous leukemia. Gleevec works by attacking the abnormal proteins made by the cancer cells.

Some scientists think it is unlikely that we will be able to repair or replace the damaged genes found in cancer cells anytime soon. Screening people for inherited cancer genes and for cancer susceptibility genes is probably technically feasible. Screening the genes of tumors for valuable information is a real possibility, as is building on the successes that have already been achieved in developing treatments aimed at knocking out the abnormal proteins made by cancer cells. From a technical standpoint, the future is very hopeful. However access to these breakthroughs in diagnosis and treatment may not be available to all people, depending on their economic status.

## POVERTY'S ROLE IN CANCER

Being poor in a rich country or living in a poor nation increases a person's cancer risk. The incidence of all cancers, except those of the breast, prostate, colon, and rectum, are higher in poor populations. In fact poverty can even be considered an underlying cause of cancer. Why is this so?

Several factors associated with cancer development are generally more prevalent among the poor, including smoking, alcohol use, poor nutrition, exposure to occupational carcinogens, and exposure to infections. Let's look at exposure to carcinogenic pathogens to highlight the overall problem. In the developing world, infectious agents are the most prevalent cause of cancer (although smoking and other forms of tobacco use are currently catching up). Many of these infections could be prevented if people had access to clean water and if municipal sanitation were improved or made available in places where it does not currently exist. Improved access to education could help people learn about ways to reduce their risks of infection and adjust their behaviors accordingly. However even if the efforts to get clean water and helpful information to people were successful, there would be a long way to go.

People need the opportunity to make a living to support their families. They need resources to provide a nutritious diet; a clean, safe place to live; and clothing to protect themselves from the elements. Without these basic necessities of life, people are more vulnerable to all types of disease, including cancer. This is not counting the high costs of delivering vaccines as they are developed, screening for cancer using the techniques we have now, and future gene screening techniques and cancer treatments as they are discovered. A significant challenge now, and for the foreseeable future is how to provide adequate living conditions, disease prevention, and disease treatment for all the people of the world.

## WHY ISN'T CANCER MORE PREVALENT?

With all that has been learned about the various factors associated with the development of cancer, the question arises why tumors don't occur in everyone. It is certainly hard to understand those cases of particular individuals who have smoked their entire lives, or worked in an asbestos mine for many years, or survived the atomic bombs at Hiroshima or Nagasaki, but did not develop cancer. How can this be?

The answer to this question is complex. Scientists have learned that multiple, interacting factors determine whether cancer will form. These factors include, but are not limited to, genetic inheritance, exposure to carcinogens, personal habits, financial situation, physiology, and chance. At the cellular level, approximately half a dozen rate-limiting, or controlling steps must occur for a tumor to become clinically discernible. In our bodies it is likely that billions of cells take the first step toward becoming cancerous, but this single step won't actually start the formation of cancer. The immune system recognizes that something is wrong with these cells and eliminates them. Many cancers may get started, but the body's defenses can usually prevent or delay the development of a full-blown malignancy.

Even when a primary tumor does develop, fewer than one in 10,000 of the cells survive to separate from that tumor to lodge elsewhere and form a secondary tumor. In addition tumors can grow only to approximately .078 inches (2 millimeters) in diameter (about one million cells) unless they get their own blood supply. The development of a malignant cancer is therefore a complicated, multistep process.

While our bodies work to thwart or stop cancer, the tumor cells that evade our defenses are those with the greatest ability to survive, proliferate, and invade other cells and tissues. They are the most dangerous. Future cancer research will be directed at preventing the formation of these advanced malignant cells early in the process, and identifying and inactivating them in situations where they have already formed. It is a race where all players—the tumor cells and the body in which they are growing—are struggling to survive.

## SUMMARY

Many questions remain regarding the causes of cancer. Research continues at an active pace. Significant avenues of inquiry include the development of vaccines for carcinogenic pathogens, chemoprevention, and screening for cancer genes. However, it needs to recognized that, for all of the technological innovation and intellectual progress being made, for many people in the developing world the biggest factor influencing their likelihood of developing cancer, or having cancer detected or treated, is poverty. In order to address the problem of cancer, the issue of poverty must be addressed in a serious way so that prevention of this disease can be a widespread reality.

# ENDNOTES

◆

1. Henschen, Folke. "Yamagiwa's Tar Cancer and Its Historical Significance." *GANN* 59 (1968): 447–451.

2. Thun, Michael J. "When Truth Is Unwelcome: The First Reports on Smoking and Lung Cancer." *Bulletin of the World Health Organization* 83, no. 2 (2005): 144–145.

3. Brickman, L. and H.D. Shapiro. "Asbestos Kills." *National Review* (January 31, 2005): 39–40.

4. Rennie, John and Ricki Rusting. "Making Headway Against Cancer." *Scientific American* 275, no. 3 (1996): 56–59.

5. Cairns, John. *Matters of Life and Death: Perspectives on Public Health, Molecular Biology, and the Prospects for the Human Race*. Princeton, N.J.: Princeton University Press, 1997, p. 257.

6. Greaves, Mel. *Cancer: The Evolutionary Legacy*. Oxford, England: Oxford University Press, 2001, p. 276.

# GLOSSARY

◆

**angiogenesis**   The growth of new blood vessels.

**angiogenic factors**   Chemicals that promote the growth of new blood vessels.

**antibiotic**   A substance that inhibits or destroys bacteria.

**asbestosis**   A chronic inflammation and disease of the lungs caused by the inhalation of asbestos fibers.

**basal cell carcinoma**   A type of skin cancer that is usually not serious and rarely metastasizes.

**benign**   Noncancerous, like a wart.

**beta-carotene**   A substance with cancer-fighting properties.

**cancer**   The uncontrolled cell proliferation and breakdown of proper cell behavior that results in the development of tumors that can spread throughout the body.

**carcinogen**   A substance that causes cancer.

**carcinogenesis**   The complex, multistep, gradual process by which cancer forms.

**cervical**   Referring to the cervix.

**cervix**   The neck of the uterus, which connects the uterus to the vagina.

**chemoprevention**   The prevention of carcinogenesis by use of natural and synthetic substances.

**chemotherapy**   The treatment of cancer with drugs.

**chromosome**   The cellular structure composed of DNA.

**cytogenetic**   Referring to the examination and analysis of the structure of chromosomes in cells.

**dengue fever**   A tropical disease, caused by a virus, in which there is a fever and pain in the joints.

**DNA** (deoxyribonucleic acid)   The substance that contains all the genetic information of a living organism.

**dysentery**   A disease causing a serious inflammation of the intestines from which severe diarrhea results.

**electron microscopy**   The use of a device that focuses an electron beam and magnifies structures as small as the parts of cells and large molecules.

**electrons**   Negatively charged subatomic particles.

**epidemiology**   The study of when and where diseases occur in a population.

**extrinsic**   External to cells or organisms.

**familial**   Refers to cancers where hereditary factors, but not a specific gene, may interact with environmental factors to produce cancer.

**filtrate**   Material passed through a filter.

**flavonoids**   An antioxidant substance found in plants.

**fluoroscopy**   A process of imaging internal organs by passing radiation through the body.

**free radical**   An atom or molecule that has an unpaired electron and is therefore unstable and highly reactive.

**gamma ray**   A high-energy type of radiation.

**gene**   Inherited instructions made up of DNA.

**gene pool** All of the genes possessed by all of the individuals within a population.

**genetic background** All of the genes possessed by an individual.

**hereditary** Refers to cancers where there is a very strong family history of the disease, in which multiple members on either side of the family and from multiple generations, develop a cancer.

**immortalized** A cell with no limit to the number of times it can divide.

**incidence** The frequency with which an event occurs.

**inflammation** A local response to tissue or cellular injury in which tissues become red, warm, and swollen.

**intrinsic** Inside a cell or organism.

**invasive** Referring to the spread of cancer cells from one part of the body to another.

**ionize** To add an electrical charge to another molecule by transferring an electron.

**leukemia** A type of cancer or malignancy that involves the white blood cells.

**light microscope** A device that focuses a light beam and magnifies objects so that we can see structures as small as bacteria.

**lymph** Bodily fluid that contains white blood cells.

**lymphoma** A type of cancer or malignancy involving the enlargement of the lymph nodes, spleen, and liver.

**malignant** Refers to cancers that grow uncontrollably and spread to other tissues in the body.

**melanoma** A highly aggressive, invasive skin cancer.

**mesothelioma**  A cancer of the pleural covering of the lungs and the peritoneum.

**metastasis**  The spread of a cancer from a primary tumor to other places in the body.

**mononucleosis**  A temporary, noncancerous infection of lymph tissue.

**mutagenic**  Causing mutations, or alterations of DNA.

**mutation**  A change or error in DNA.

**nasopharyngeal**  Refers to the nose and pharynx, the cavity behind the mouth and nose.

**oncogenic**  Causing cancer.

**pacemaker**  A device for stimulating the heart muscle and controlling the heartbeat.

**Pap tests**  Medical tests done to screen for cervical lesions, precancerous growths, or cancer of the cervix.

**pathogen**  Something, such as bacteria or a virus, that causes a disease.

**pedigree**  A family tree that records the genetics of parents and offspring over many generations.

**perinatally**  Occurring within a few months before birth to a few months after birth.

**peritoneum**  The lining of the abdominal cavity.

**phytochemicals**  Chemicals that are isolated from plants.

**pleural covering**  A membrane that covers the lungs and lines the thoracic cavity.

**polyp**  A growth that projects from the surface of a tissue.

**radiation**  Energy transmitted as waves, rays, or particles.

**radiation therapy**  The treatment of cancer with radiation.

**radioactive**  The emission of radiation from atoms.

**radon**   A radioactive gas that can seep from the earth into mines or underground spaces.

**remission**   A decrease or cessation of a disease that may be temporary.

**retinoblastoma**   A childhood cancer of the retina, the light-gathering structure of the eye.

**retinoids**   Substances related to vitamin A that have cancer-fighting properties.

**sarcoma**   A type of cancer of bone, muscle, or connective tissue.

**schistosomes**   Parasitic flatworms.

**scrotum**   The skin that encloses the testes.

**sporadic**   Refers to cases of cancer where there was no family history of the disease.

**squamous cell carcinoma**   A type of skin cancer that sometimes spreads elsewhere in the body.

**tissue culture**   The growth of groups of cells or tissues outside of the body in petri dishes or flasks.

**transform**   To change from a healthy cell to a cancerous one.

**tuberculosis**   An infectious lung disease.

**tumor**   An abnormal mass of cells.

**tumor suppressor**   A substance that stops the growth and development of a tumor.

**typhus**   An infectious disease transmitted by fleas, mites, or lice that is characterized by high fever, severe headaches, delirium, and a rash.

**ultraviolet (UV) light**   A type of radiation that has higher energy than visible light but less energy than X rays.

**virus**   A parasite that is much smaller than a cell.

**X ray**   A relatively high-energy form of radiation.

# FURTHER RESOURCES

◆

## Bibliography

Arnold, Robert. "Environmental Contamination and Cancer Rates." *Journal of Environmental Engineering* (August 2002): 669–671.

Attanoos, R. L., D. H. Thomas, and A. R. Gibbs. "Synchronous Diffuse Malignant Mesothelioma and Carcinomas in Asbestos-exposed Individuals." *Histopathology* 43 (2003): 387–392.

Bass, Thomas. "Mary-Claire King." *Omni* 15, no. 9 (1993): 68–73.

Bennett, Ian C., Michael Gattas, and Bin Tean Teh. "The Genetic Basis of Breast Cancer and Its Clinical Observations." *ANZ Journal of Surgery.* 69 (1999): 95–105.

Benowitz, Steven I. *Cancer.* Berkeley Heights, N.J.: Enslow Publishers, Inc., 1999.

Bishop, J. Michael. *How to Win the Nobel Prize.* Cambridge, Mass.: Harvard University Press, 2003.

Bonn, Dorothy. "Evidence for the Link Between Magnetic Fields and Cancer Weak at Most." *The Lancet* 353 (1999): 2217.

Brickman, Lester, and Harvey D. Shapiro. "Asbestos Kills—And More Than Just People: Jobs, Ethics, and Elementary Justice." *National Review* (January 31, 2005): 39–41.

Cairns, John. *Matters of Life and Death: Perspectives on Public Health, Molecular Biology, Cancer, and the Prospects for the Human Race.* Princeton, N.J.: Princeton University Press, 1997.

Children's Hospital Boston. "Judah Folkman, M.D." Available online. URL: http://web1.tch.harvard.edu/cfapps/research/data_admin/Site105/mainpageS105P0.html. Accessed March 2, 2007.

Cook, Christopher. "Oral History—Sir Richard Doll." *Journal of Public Health* 26, 4 (2004): 327–336.

Cooper, Geoffrey M. *The Cell: A Molecular Approach*, 2nd ed. Washington, D.C.: ASM Press, 2000.

Darby, Sarah. "A Conversation with Sir Richard." *Epidemiology* 14, no. 3 (2003): 375–379.

DiMagno, Eugene P. "Lifetime Achievement Award: Henry Lynch, M.D. International Symposium on Inherited Diseases of the Pancreas." *Genetic Disorders of the Exocrine Pancreas*. Basel, Switzerland: Karger Publishers, 2002, pp. 149–153. Also available online. URL: http://content.karger.com/ProdukteDB/produkte.asp?typ=pdf&doi=70356. Accessed March 2, 2007.

DNAdirect: Your Genes in Context. "Breast and Ovarian Cancer: How Are Breast and Ovarian Cancer Inherited?" Available online. URL: http://www.dnadirect.com/resource/conditions/breast_cancer/GH_Brca_. Accessed July 7, 2005.

Dockerty, John D., J. Mark Elwood, David C. G. Skegg, and G. Peter Harrison. "Electromagnetic Field Exposures and Childhood Leukemia in New Zealand." *The Lancet* 354 (1999): 1967–1968.

Duffy, Christine, and Michele Cyr. "The Relationship Among Alcohol, Folate and Breast Cancer Risk." *The Brown University Digest of Addiction Theory & Application* 24, no. 30 (2005): 8.

Dumitrescu, R. G., and I. Cotarla. "Understanding Breast Cancer Risk—Where Do We Stand in 2005?" *Journal of Cellular and Molecular Medicine* 9, no. 1 (2005): 208–211.

El-Omar, Emad M. "*Helicobacter pylori* in Gastric Cancer." *The Royal College of Surgeons*. Available online. URL: http://www.edu.rcsed.ac.uk/lectures/lt19.htm. Accessed March 9, 2007.

Enerson, Ole Daniel. "Henry T. Lynch." Available online. URL: http://www.whonamedit.com/doctor.cfm/1970.html. Accessed March 9, 2007.

Ewald, Paul W. *Plague Time: The New Germ Theory of Disease*. New York: Anchor Books, 2002.

Eye Cancer Network. "Retinoblastoma." Available online. URL: http://www.eyecancer.com/conditions/Retinal%20Tumors/retino.html. Accessed July 7, 2005.

———. "Retinoblastoma and Secondary Cancers." Available online. URL: http://www.eyecancer.com/conditions/Retinal%20Tumors/retinos.html. Accessed July 7, 2005.

———. "Retinoblastoma Genetics." Available online. URL: http://www.eyecancer.com/conditions/Retinal%20Tumors/retinog.html. Accessed July 7, 2005.

French, Peter W., Ronald Penny, Jocelyn A. Laurence, and David R. McKenzie. "Mobile Phones, Heat Shock Proteins and Cancer." *Differentiation* 67 (2000): 93–97.

Gibbs, W. Wayt. "Untangling the Roots of Cancer." *Scientific American* 289, no. 1 (2003): 56–65.

Greaves, Mel. *Cancer: The Evolutionary Legacy.* Oxford, England: Oxford University Press, 2001.

Greenwald, Peter. "Chemoprevention of Cancer." *Scientific American* 275, no. 3 (1996): 96–99.

Hahn, William C., and Robert A. Weinberg. "Rules for Making Human Tumor Cells." *New England Journal of Medicine* 347, no. 920 (2002): 1593–1603.

Harper, Clive G., and Victor K. Lee. "Editorial: Mobile Phones and Your Health." *Pathology* 33 (2001): 269–270.

Hemminki, Kari. "Genetic Epidemiology: Science and Ethics on Familial Cancers." *Acta Oncologica* 40, no. 4 (2001): 439–444.

Henschen, Folke. "Yamagiwa's Tar Cancer and Its Historical Significance—From Percival Pott to Katsusaburo Yamagiwa." *GANN* 59 (1968): 447–451.

Hieger, I., and G. M. Badger. "Ernest Laurence Kennaway 23rd May 1881–1st January 1958." *Journal of Path. Bact.* 78 (1959): 593–606.

Hood, Ernie. "Passing Along Pesticides: Lymphoma Rises in Children of Applicators." *Environmental Health Perspectives* 112, no. 5 (2004): A300.

Ingraham, John L., and Catherine A. Ingraham. *Introduction to Microbiology,* 2nd Ed. Pacific Grove, Calif.: Brooks/Cole Thompson Learning, 2000.

Joshi, Tushar K., and Rohit Gupta. "Asbestos in Developing Countries: Magnitude of Risk and Its Practical Implications." *Human and Ecological Risk Assessment* 11(2005): 239–247.

"Katsusaburo Yamagiwa (1863-1930)." *CA—A Cancer Journal for Clinicians* 27, no. 3 (1977): 172–173.

Kuper, H., H.-O. Adami, and D. Trichopoulos. "Infections as a Major Preventable Cause of Cancer." *Journal of Internal Medicine* 248 (2000): 171–183.

Lai, P.K., and J. Roy. "Antimicrobial and Chemopreventative Properties of Herbs and Spices." *Current Medicinal Chemistry* 11 (2004): 1451–1460.

Leaf, Clifton. "The War on Cancer." *Fortune.com.* Available online. URL: http://www.http://money.cnn.com/magazines/fortune/fortune_archive/2004/03/22/365076/index.html. Accessed March 9, 2007.

Lee, Ki Won, Hyong Joo Lee, and Chang Yong Lee. "Vitamins, Phytochemicals, Diets, and Their Implementation in Cancer Prevention." *Critical Reviews in Food Science and Nutrition* 44 (2004): 437–452.

Legge, Robert T. "Industrial Medicine's Hall of Fame: Percival Pott, F.R.S." *Industrial Medicine and Surgery* 9 (1955): 419–420.

Leiss, Jack K., and David A. Savitz. "Home Pesticide Use and Childhood Cancer: A Case-Control Study." *American Journal of Public Health* 85, no. 2 (1995): 249–252.

Little, C. C. "John Joseph Bittner 1904–1961." *Oncology* 16 (1963): 354–356.

Mercat-Rommens, Catherine, Didier Louvat, Celine Duffa, and Anne Sugier. "Comparison Between Radiological and Chemical Health Risks Assessments: The Nord-Cotentin Study." *Human and Ecological Risk Assessment* 11 (2005): 627–644.

Michaels, David. "When Science Isn't Enough: Wilhelm Hueper, Robert A. M. Case, and the Limits of Scientific Evidence in Preventing Occupational Bladder Cancer." *International Journal of Occupational and Environmental Health* 1 (1995): 278–288.

Mustacchi, Piero, and Michael B. Shimkin. "Radiation Cancer and Jean Clunet." *Cancer* 9 (1956): 1073–1074.

National Cancer Institute, National Institutes of Health. "Genetics of Breast and Ovarian Cancer: Health Professional Version." Available online. URL: http://nci.nih.gov/cancertopics/pdq/genetics/breast-and-ovarian/. Accessed July 8, 2005.

————, National Institutes of Health. "Retinoblastoma." Available online. URL: http://www.meb.uni-bonn.de/cancer.gov/CDR0000062846.html. Accessed July 7, 2005.

National Eye Institute, National Institutes of Health. "Retinoblastoma." Available online. URL: http://www.ncbi.nlm.nih.gov/disease/Retinoblast.html. Accessed July 7, 2005.

National Foundation for Cancer Research. "Michael Sporn, M.D." Available online. URL: http://www.nfcr.org/default.aspx?tabid=359. Accessed July 7, 2005.

National Library of Medicine, National Institutes of Health. "The C. Everett Koop Papers: Biographical Information." Available online. URL: http://profiles.nlm.nih.gov/QQ/Views/Exhibit/narrative/biographical.html. Accessed August 8, 2005.

————. "The C. Everett Koop Papers: Tobacco, Second-Hand Smoke, and the Campaign for a Smoke-Free America." Available online. URL: http://profiles.nlm.nih.gov/QQ/Views/Exhibit/narrative/tobacco.html. Accessed August 8, 2005.

Nelson, Heather, and Karl T. Kelsey. "The Molecular Epidemiology of Asbestos and Tobacco in Lung Cancer." *Oncogene* 21 (2002): 7284–7288.

Nicol, Alcina Frederica, Ana Teresa Gomes Fernandes, and Maria da Gloria Bonecini-Almeida. "Immune Response in Cervical Dysplasia Induced by Human Papillomavirus: The Influence of Human Immunodeficiency Virus-1 Co-infection—Review." *Memorias do Instituto Oswaldo Cruz, Rio de Janeiro* 100, no. 1 (2005): 1–12.

Nobelprize.org. "Hermann J. Muller—Biography." Available online. URL: http://nobelprize.org/medicine/laureates/1946/muller-bio.html. Accessed August 2, 2005.

————. "Peyton Rous—Biography." Available online. URL: http://nobelprize.org/medicine/laureates/1966/rous-bio.html. Accessed January 17, 2005.

Nova Online, Public Broadcasting System (PBS). "Dr. Folkman Speaks." Available online. URL: http://www.pbs.org/wgbh/nova/cancer/folkman.html. Accessed February 4, 2005.

Paustenbach, Dennis J., Brent L. Finley, Elizabeth T. Lu, Gregory P. Brorby, and Patrick J. Sheehan. "Environmental and Occupational Health Hazards Associated With The Presences of Asbestos in Brake Linings and Pads (1900 to Present): A "State-of-the-Art" Review." *Journal of Toxicology and Environmental Health,* Part B 7 (2004): 33–110.

Pelucchi, C., M. Malvezzi, C. LaVecchia, F. Levi, A. Decarli and E. Negri. "The Mesothelioma Epidemic in Western Europe: An Update." *British Journal of Cancer* 90 (2004): 1022–1024.

Peto, Julian. "Cancer Epidemiology in the Last Century and the Next Decade." *Nature* 444 (2001): 390–395.

Pickrell, John. "Cancer Causer?" *Science News* 162, no. 11 (2002): 179–180.

Raloff, Janet. "Study Can't Tie EMFs to Cancer." *Science News* 167, no. 9 (2005): 142.

Rennie, John, and Ricki Rusting. "Making Headway Against Cancer." *Scientific American* 275, no. 3 (1996): 56–59.

Retinoblastoma International. "Children's Stories." Available online. URL: http://www.retinoblastoma.net/children.html. Accessed July 7, 2005.

————. "What Is Retinoblastoma?" Available online. URL: http://www.retinoblastoma.net/whatisrb.html. Accessed July 7, 2005.

Ron, Elaine, Takayoshi Ikeda, Dale R. Preston, and Shoji Tokuoka. "Male Breast Cancer Incidence Among Atomic Bomb Survivors." *Journal of the National Cancer Institute* 97, no. 8 (2005): 603–605.

Saraiya, Mona, Karen Glanz, Peter Briss, Phyllis Nichols, Cornelia White, and Debjani Das. "Preventing Skin Cancer: Findings of the Task Force on Community Preventative Services on Reducing Exposure to Ultraviolet Light." *Morbidity and Mortality Weekly Report* 52 (2003): 1–12.

Schubert, Charlotte. "Mary-Claire King." *Nature Medicine* 9, no. 6 (2003): 633.

Scientific American.com. "Quiet Celebrity: Interview with Judah Folkman." Available online. URL: http://www.sciam.com/print_version. cfm?articleID=00077C61-DE6E-1DC2-AF71809EC5. Accessed February 4, 2005.

Shand, William. "Percival Pott, FRS (1716–1788)." *Trauma* 2 (2000): 291–295.

Stewart, Harold L. "Spoken on the Occasion of the National Institutes of Health Director's Award to Dr. Wilhelm C. Hueper on Friday, September 1, 1978." *Journal of the National Cancer Institute* 62, no. 4 (1979): 719–721.

Thun, Michael J. "When Truth Is Unwelcome: The First Reports on Smoking and Lung Cancer." *Bulletin of the World Health Organization* 83, no. 2 (2005): 144–145.

Tran, H. K. Chen, and S. Shumack. "Epidemiology and Aetiology of Basal Cell carcinoma." *British Journal of Dermatology* 149 (2003): 50–52.

Trichopoulos, Dimitrios, Frederick P. Li, and David J. Hunter. "What Causes Cancer?" *Scientific American* 275, no. 3 (1996): 80–87.

Victorian Lace-Victorian Lifestyle. "Innocence Lost . . . The Sad Side of 19th-Century Childhood." Available online. URL: http://www.geocities.com/ victorian lace12/innocence.html. Accessed January 26, 2005.

Weschsler-Reya, Robert, and Matthew P. Scott. "The Developmental Biology of Brain Tumors." *Annual Review of Neuroscience* 24 (2001): 385–428.

"What You Need to Know About Cancer." *Scientific American* 275, no. 3 (1996): 56–167.

Willett, Walter C., Graham A. Colditz, and Nancy E. Mueller. "Strategies for Minimizing Risk." *Scientific American* 275, no. 3 (1996): 88–95.

Yount, Lisa. *Cancer.* Belmont, CA: Thompson Gale, 2000.

## Web Sites

### American Cancer Society (ACS)
http://www.cancer.org/

### Cancer BACUP
http://www.cancerbacup.org.uk/
Europe's leading cancer information service

### Centers for Disease Control and Prevention (CDC)
http://www.cdc.gov

### National Cancer Institute
http://www.cancer.gov
http://www.nci.nih.gov/cancertopics

# INDEX

♦

# ABOUT THE AUTHOR

◆

**DONNA M. BOZZONE** earned her B.S. in biology from Manhattan College in 1978 and her M.A. and Ph.D. in biology, from Princeton University in 1980 and 1983, respectively. She continued her education as a postdoctoral research associate at the Worcester Foundation for Experimental Biology. She joined the faculty of Saint Michael's College in 1987 and she is now professor of biology.

Dr. Bozzone's areas of specialization are in developmental and cellular biology. She teaches, or has taught, courses in introductory biology, science writing, cell biology, developmental biology, genetics, plant developmental physiology, and a senior seminar on the history of biology. An author of more than 25 publications, Dr. Bozzone is also a member of the Publication Review Panel for the *Journal of College Science Teaching* and an *ad hoc* reviewer for *American Biology Teacher*. An enthusiast for science education at all levels, Dr. Bozzone designs laboratory teaching materials for students in high school and college, and also works with students who are training to become biology teachers. She and her husband, Douglas Green, who is also a biology professor at Saint Michael's, live in Vermont with their two teenage daughters.